The Kid's ROTH IRA Handbook

The Kid's ROTH IRA Handbook

Securing Tax-Free Wealth from a Child's First Paycheck

OR

Money Answers for Employed Children, Their Parents, The Self-Employed and Entrepreneurs

TRACY FOOTE
TracyTrends
New York, USA

To:
My family

First printing
Printed in the United States of America
Cover Design: Peri Poloni-Gabriel, Knockout Design
www.knockoutbooks.com
Text Copyright © 2008 by Tracy Foote
Illustration Copyright © 2008 by Tracy Foote
Published by TracyTrends
www.TracyTrends.com

This book may be purchased in bulk orders for classroom lessons.
Please send all inquiries to:
TracyTrends
c/o T. Foote
27 West 86 St, Suite 17B
New York, NY 10024
tracytrends@aol.com

ISBN 10: 0-9708226-9-3
ISBN 13: 978-0-9708226-9-7
Library of Congress Control Number: 2007909236
To suggest updates to this book visit:
www.TracyTrends.com/books/kid-roth-ira.html
To check for new information on child roth IRAs visit:
www.TracyTrends.com/books/child-roth-ira-updates.html
For more resources visit:
www.TracyTrends.com/teach-kid-money.html

No Substitute
For Professional Guidance

This book is to be used as a starting point for children and parents to understand:
- benefits of a Roth IRA
- different types of child employment
- different ways parents can employ their children
- how parents can issue Forms W-2 for their children
- basic taxes for children with low earned income
- rules for children to contribute to a Roth IRA

The focus is the unmarried dependent child (with no dependents of his or her own), with no investment income (stocks, mutual funds, etc. generating taxable unearned income in the child's name), who has a yearly income that ranges from $1.00 to the amount of the single standard deduction allowed by the Internal Revenue Service for the current tax year ($5,350 in 2007).

This book can also provide limited guidance for children with incomes outside of this range. However, such children will need to obtain further consultation on the different circumstances that will apply to them.

This book provides a solid foundation for a basic understanding of the many issues surrounding child employment, taxes, and Roth IRAs. By building your knowledge of the basics, when you do need consultations with financial experts, discussions will be less time consuming, more easily understood, and less expensive for you.

Every effort has been made to ensure that all statements can be documented and are current as of the printing date. However, information in this book is not a substitute for informed professional guidance on tax, legal, investment, accounting, or any other type of specialized advice. It is sold with the understanding that you will not hold the author or publisher liable for any losses, damages, or alleged losses or damages attributed to information within and that you will seek professional assistance appropriate to your own unique circumstances.

Table of Contents

Preface

I wrote this book as a starting point for children and parents to become educated on how to start a Roth IRA from the very first paycheck. I hope it instills the sense of urgency that once kids have a job, the next immediate step is to begin a Roth IRA. I encourage readers to use this book as a learning tool to show the many ways children can be employed today and as a quick reference guide to publications needed from the IRS to assist in tax completion and law clarification.

Let's teach kids that lost opportunity can be both financially and emotionally painful. Lost means gone! You can never get it back again. Every year they wait to start a Roth IRA, they lose another opportunity for tax-free compounded earnings and they can never get that opportunity back.

Let's also remember that children constantly surprise us. In completing research for this book, I found reviews (written by young children) of related investment books, complaining that the text was much too simple and the book was written for a beginner, someone who knew nothing about money. This book covers some very basic ideas but quickly moves into complex issues. We should not presume children will not look at a tax publication but instead be optimistic and provide them with the opportunity and incentive to do so.

With the pace in which the appeal of the internet is growing each day, it is not unreasonable to direct kids to use links or online calculators to project their finances. Children learn quickly, enjoy challenges and think computers are fun. As parents, we should assist them, guide them, teach them, and set a good example through our own financial behavior.

I recommend using this book as an interactive guide between parents and children.

Tracy Foote

How to Use this Handbook

The text is written speaking to the child, making it easier for children to read. As a reference book, some minor repetition occurs to benefit those who choose to read by specific topic. However, but tax must be read in order as instructions build on one another.

This book has three main areas of interest:

- The different types of possible employment for kids
- Information about the Roth IRA and related issues
- Tax forms related to employed children

Parents should:

- Use the sections on different types of jobs to assist their child in obtaining some sort of earned income so their child can contribute to a Roth IRA
- Pre-read the types of jobs before their child so they can answer any questions their child may have
- Consider employing their child if they own their own business. (Special tax rules exist for sole proprietorship or a partnership business, where the spouse is the partner.)
- Consider employing their child as a household employee
- Pre-read the Roth IRA sections and use them as a tool to explain tax-free compounding earnings to their child
- Assist their child in opening a Roth IRA for a minor and assist their child in choosing the type of security for the Roth investment (such as a simple money market account, bonds, mutual funds, or stocks)
- When tax time arrives, assist their child with his or her local, state, and federal taxes using the tax guidance provided in this book (along with IRS publications and state instruction booklets) as well as a tax professional for any unique circumstances

Kids should:

- Read the job sections in the book to understand the types of employment possibilities that can create the earned income needed to invest in a Roth IRA
- Take advantage of multiple resources (including their school librarian, guidance counselor, family, friends, local librarian, newspapers, and help wanted posters) around them to begin looking for a type of future employment that might interest them
- Try to attend any employment type class offered at school (such as a babysitting safe-sitter class) because some skills learned there will be relevant to all types of jobs, the class will give kids qualifications (training experience) to list when applying for a job, and taking classes shows maturity, responsibility, and initiative
- Read the Roth IRA sections and related issues to fully understand the value of tax-free compounding interest and why they should choose a Roth IRA as the best savings investment for their hard earned money
- Ask parents or teachers for assistance and advice
- Read the sections on taxes, before they begin working, especially the section applicable to their specific type of employment, so they will have no surprises when tax time comes next year

Both Parents and Kids should:

- Learn to move back and forth from one section of the book to another. This is a great skill to develop, to be able to go from one area to another when more information is needed. This will be a helpful skill when you actually have to read an IRS publication which will frequently move you from section to another.

The Decision

Has anyone ever asked you, "What do you want to be when you grow up?" Usually they expect you to answer with some type of profession: fireman, doctor, teacher, artist, or any other job that interests you.

I bet you would surprise them if you answered, "I want to be financially stable." That is an answer that Grandma, your teacher, or whoever is asking you would not expect. I bet you would have an interesting conversation following that comment, especially if you share the ideas you will learn about in this book.

Well, what does it mean to have "financial stability?"

> **Financial Stability:** When you have financial stability, you do not rely on anyone for money and have emergency funds for any unforeseen events that could occur in everyday life.

This book shows you how you can use an IRA, an Individual Retirement Account (which is a type of financial investment) to start becoming financially stable.

Why do you care about being financially stable? Why do you need this? Are you thinking right now that you have parents to take care of you, so you don't need this book?

Right now, you are *financially dependent* on your parents. You rely on them. But, let's remember that your parents will not be there forever. You will hopefully pursue an education, move out of the house, and buy your own home someday.

You have your own dreams and your own vision of what you want to achieve in the world. If you start early to become financially stable, life will definitely be less stressful for you, and this should allow you time for more fun! That's what this book is about – starting off on the right foot.

Making the right decision is very important. One you have money, whether it is from your birthday or a part time job, you have to make a decision. The decision you need to make is: What will you do with your money? Your choices are: spend all of it, save all of it, donate all of it, or spend part, save part and donate part. This book recommends saving at least part of your earned money in a Roth IRA.

The reason you need to decide to begin saving immediately is the later you start saving, the less time your money will have to grow.

Let's look at an example to explain this. Let's think of your money like a garden. The later your garden is started, the less time it has to grow because winter is right around the corner.

The farmer who *starts early* and plants his seeds in March may harvest his first tomato in July. He has tomatoes growing from July until September. He has so many tomatoes, he freezes some and still has extra to give to his friends to enjoy. He makes tomato sauce and eats pasta all winter long. He has so much food that he invites his neighbors to have dinner with him. This all happened because he started early.

Now, the farmer who *starts later,* and plants his seeds in June, harvests his first tomato in late August. He has to use his tomatoes sparingly to be sure he has some to freeze to make pasta sauce during the winter. His growing season is shorter because he started late. He has a few more concerns because of the *lost time*!

The longer you wait to begin saving in a Roth IRA, the more time has been lost. It is a *lost opportunity* for your money to grow. You cannot have that time, that opportunity, back again. It is gone forever.

So, you are losing time right now. But we are going to change this. We are going to become educated first and then take the necessary steps to make sure we are maximizing our opportunities, maximizing our time, so we will have the greatest wealth possible, or as the farmer would say, "The greatest harvest."

Your next question should be, "What is a Roth IRA and how do I open one?" And that is what this book will help answer. It will help put you on the road to financial independence and financial stability.

First, you are going to learn a lot. Imagine the farmer who didn't know any better and planted his tomatoes in January. He was so surprised and disappointed when the frost came and destroyed his plants. So, he decided to become educated. He learned about the best time to begin his seeds. He learned techniques to start growing seeds indoors before the outdoor growing season began. Later, he transplanted these tomatoes when there was no fear of frost. This procedure increased his growing season giving him more time to harvest and the result was a huge crop of tomatoes lasting through the winter. Education makes a difference.

Farmers continue their education all the time, reading about new gardening facts to grow even better tomatoes. They might learn of a tomato breed that will resist insects so they choose that breed because it will mean many more tomatoes which will be much more profitable! Sounds great!

You too will continue your education, beyond reading this book. But this book is the beginning. It is the start down the right path, the path to understanding tax-free wealth.

So, what is an IRA? Technically an IRA is an Individual Retirement *Arrangement*, but most people refer to it as an Individual Retirement *Account*, which is a true statement, just not the true definition of the abbreviation. Through out this book we will also refer to an IRA as an Individual Retirement Account.

The Internal Revenue Service (IRS) defines many of the terms used in employment, accounting, and tax issues.

> **IRA**: "An IRA is a personal savings plan that gives you tax advantages for setting aside money for retirement."[1]

These tax advantages are important as you start earning income. *Earned income* is the money you receive for working.

So, how do you open a Roth IRA? The first thing you need is earned income which as I said is money you receive from working. This means you need to have some sort of a job. You absolutely *must* have earned income to open up an IRA account. The law requires it.

The first sections of this book will discuss the many job opportunities for you and the issues that surround these jobs. Then the book moves into the details, the reasons to choose a Roth IRA. In the last sections, the book will look at taxes and how the rules apply to children with lower incomes.

Let's start with you. Why did you buy this book? Perhaps you are thinking about obtaining a job. Perhaps you already have a job and heard about this retirement savings called an IRA and you want to know how to begin. Or, perhaps this book is a gift from your parents. However you got hold of it, this book will be a good reference tool for you.

As we go through this book, you will find references to Internal Revenue Service (IRS) publications that will confirm the information explained in this book. You don't have to rely on taking my word for it. While this book ties together all of the important issues, the relevant laws are expressed in the IRS documents. You need to be aware of the IRS documents the book has used so you know where to look to check if the current law has changed. This will be easy for you to do because I will tell you exactly where to look. Let's get started!

---

[1] *IRS Publication 590, Individual Retirement Arrangement*

Where is Your Money?

Do you have some money already? Maybe you received money as a birthday gift or for achieving good grades in school, or maybe your parents give you a weekly allowance.

What do you do with your money?

Or, if you do not have money, what would you do with money if you had some?

When you were age 6, maybe you would use money to buy some candy. At age 10, some kids would want to use money for a video game. What do kids want at age 17? Maybe seventeen year olds would want a car.

We all have goals of things we would like to buy. Adults have their list of goals too which might include a car, a house, or a vacation trip. So, when it comes to money, kids and adults are very similar. We all think we could use a little more money to buy that item on our list!

Adults and kids are similar in other ways too. When adults want to purchase an item, they need to save their money until they have enough to buy it. Kids and adults have the same question to answer, "What should I do with my money? Save it, donate it to a charity, or spend it?"

You may have heard the childhood rhyme:

Good, Better, Best,
Never Let it Rest,
Until the Good Gets Better,
And the Better Gets Best.

Well, the *Good* is your piggy bank in your home. It is good to save your money in a safe place. You can keep adding more money to it and the total balance will grow. Eventually, over time, you will have enough money saved for the item you want.

The *Better* is a savings account in a bank. Once you have saved a significant amount of money in your piggy bank, you should open a savings account. When you open a savings account in a bank, the bank pays you interest.

Interest: is what someone pays you for having the use of your money.

You give your money to a bank and the bank pays you for letting them use your money.

Does it surprise you that the bank is using your money? This means when you deposit a $10 bill, you will not receive the exact same $10 bill back at withdrawal time. In fact, the bank could give you ten $1 bills back!

What do you think the bank did with your original $10 bill? How is the bank using your money?

When you deposit your money into a bank, the bank promises to give you the money back with interest each month you leave it in the bank. (By depositing your money in the bank, you are using your money to make more money.)

But the bank needs to make money too. The bank will loan your money out to someone else who needs it. It could be someone buying a car, starting a business, or someone needing money for something else.

When the bank loans money, the bank charges the person receiving the money a high interest rate. The interest will be much higher than what the bank promised to pay you.

The bank will keep the difference between the interest it pays you and the interest it receives from the person who took the loan. This is how the bank uses your money to make money for the bank.

The diagram example illustrates how the bank uses your money and how the bank makes money for itself!

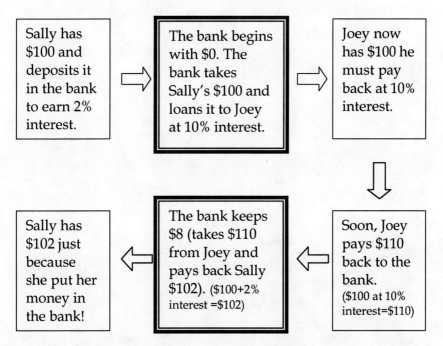

Sally has $100 and deposits it in the bank to earn 2% interest.	The bank begins with $0. The bank takes Sally's $100 and loans it to Joey at 10% interest.	Joey now has $100 he must pay back at 10% interest.
Sally has $102 just because she put her money in the bank!	The bank keeps $8 (takes $110 from Joey and pays back Sally $102). ($100+2% interest =$102)	Soon, Joey pays $110 back to the bank. ($100 at 10% interest=$110)

Sally is happy because now she has $102 just for leaving her money in the bank. Her money made her more money. Joey is happy because he was able to buy something using the bank loan (even though it cost him 10% interest). And, the bank is happy because it received $8 just for helping Sally and Joey. ($110 from Joey minus $102 from Sally = $8 for the bank.) This is how banks make money.

Even small amounts of money can earn money. If you put $10 in a savings account that pays 5% interest for the year, at the end of the year you will have $10.50. The bank paid you .50 for letting them hold and use your money. By not spending your money and putting it in a bank, you are actually making money! How cool is that?

So if you are employed, if you have a job that pays you, when you deposit your pay into the bank and go hang out with your friends, your money is making money! Would you rather make money by working more or would you rather make money when you are talking to friends?

Let's look at that thought again:

Would you rather make money by working more or would you rather make money when you are talking to friends?

We want to make money without working. That sounds great!

The piggy bank was good because you were saving your money but the bank is better because it pays you interest for just leaving your money there.

Also, when your money is in a savings account you will benefit from compounding interest.

Compounding Interest: Compounding interest means you will earn interest on interest you have previously earned.

Let's look closer at the cartoon of Sally and her friend. Sally said, "I'm making money" when she was eating French fries. Sally put $20 in her bank savings account in January and it earned 10% interest every month. (Most banks earn much less than 10% but this will make the numbers very easy for us to see how everything works.)

In January, Sally had a balance of $20. On February 1, Sally will have a balance of $22. This is because she received $2 in interest (10% of $20 = $2) from the bank on her $20 deposit. We add that together $20 + $2 to arrive at $22.

Sally now earns interest on the interest earned in January. So in February, Sally will now earn 10% interest on her new balance of $22.

At the end of February, Sally will have $22 + $2.20 interest from the bank for a total of $24.20. (We computed 10% interest on $22 to give us $2.20 for the amount of interest Sally earned in February. Then we added $2.20 to her $22 balance she had at the beginning of the month.) Sally earned more interest in February because the bank paid her interest on the interest she earned in January! This repeats monthly!

	Jan	Feb	Mar	Apr
Balance	$20.00	$22.00	$24.20	$26.62
10% Interest	$ 2.00	$ 2.20	$ 2.42	$ 2.66

If Sally leaves all her money in the bank, we can see the compounding of interest is making Sally even more money. Her money is making money.

If you like to do math, take some paper and work the figures to see how much Sally would earn if she left $100 in the bank for 12 months, earning 10% compounding interest per month. You would see that Sally will earn even more money because she put more money in at the beginning.

This interest that you earn in the bank savings account is taxed by the government. Taxes pay for things like repairing roads and other things the government provides. Taxes are necessary for our country. Even though no one likes to pay them, we want our roads fixed (among other things) so taxes are a part of everyday life.

How do taxes relate to your savings?

Imagine if you have a $1,000 dollars in your savings account. You will earn a lot more interest because you have more money in your account. At a 5% annual interest rate, you will earn $50 for the year. Well, by law, savings account interest is taxable, so part of that $50 will be taxed if you file your taxes for that year.

If you put the same money, $1,000 into a Roth IRA and it earned 5% interest, you would also have an additional $50 at the end of the year. But, in this case, the $50 is not taxable! A Roth IRA grows tax free! You get to keep all of your money!

Remember the children's rhyme *Good, Better, Best*? Start with your piggy bank which is good, then open a savings account which is better, and then open a Roth IRA, which is the best! If you follow the guidance of this book you will have both a savings account and a Roth IRA account. Use the savings account to save for small purchases and the Roth IRA to save for long term.

As stated previously, the first thing you need to contribute to a Roth IRA is earned income or money you received from working. This means you will need to obtain some form of employment. You cannot use your birthday money or weekly allowance.

Let's cover that idea in the next few sections. Let's see the different ways kids are able to receive earned income.

Obtaining Earned Income

What Type of Job Can You Do?

Remember the first step is to obtain the earned income needed to contribute to an IRA, which means getting some sort of employment, a paying job.

There are child labor laws in the United States to protect you and other children. The laws protect your right to health, safety and an education. This means the laws are designed to ensure you have time to receive a good education, you are not overworked (working excessive hours during the day) and that you will not be in harms way when working.

The Department of Labor[2] sets the federal rules for child labor here in the United States. Your state may also have labor rules you must follow. Try asking your school guidance counselor if you have one, school librarian, or local librarian for information on your state's child labor laws.

If you choose to be self-employed, the child labor laws do not apply to you because you are working for yourself.

Generally, if you are under age 14, you are not allowed to work for someone else unless the job falls under a list of exceptions. Exceptions include newspaper delivery, casual babysitting, and household work in and around private homes (like cleaning or lawn mowing). You can also work in radio, television, movie or theatrical productions. After all, look at the kids on TV and the babies modeling on covers of magazines. Another exception is you may work for your parents if the work is not a mining, a manufacturing or an occupation that has an age requirement of 18 or older.[3]

---

[2] www.dol.gov/dol/topic/youthlabor/index.htm
[3] www.dol.gov/dol/topic/youthlabor/employmentparents.htm

Children ages 14 and 15 are also protected by restrictions on the time of day they may begin and end working, as well as the total number of hours they are allowed to work each week. Limits include: 3 hours on a school day (18 hours in a school week), 8 hours on a non-school day (40 hours in a non-school week), and hours from 7 a.m. to 7 p.m. (except June 1 through Labor Day where work hours are extend to 9 p.m.).

Well, who's going to hire you? What will be your first job? Below is a list of jobs children through young adults can do.

- acting
- artist
- babysitter
- cashier
- camp counselor
- cook
- dog walker
- elderly assistant
- filing
- gardening
- grocery bagging
- household cleaning
- lawn mowing
- lemonade stand
- modeling
- moving assistant
- musician
- newspaper delivery
- office assistant
- painter
- party assistant
- pet-sitter
- pizza delivery
- plant sitter
- raking leaves
- recycling assistant
- restaurant bus boy
- selling baked goods
- selling craft items
- street entertainer (singing, break dancing, clown, etc.)
- stuffing envelopes
- ticket taker (movie, museum, etc.)
- tutoring
- waitress
- water gardens
- writer - traditional
- writer - self-publisher
- window cleaner

Don't worry about picking a job right now. The list is for ideas. This purpose of this book is not to make you go out and get a job, but to give you ideas about working and to educate you about *what you should do once you do have a job.*

Job Type 1: Employer — Employee Relationship

Let's look at the type of job where there is a relationship between an employer and an employee. Let's call this type, the Employer — Employee relationship. The employer is the boss, the one who sets the work hours. The employer gives you a job description describing tasks you are to complete.

A good example of an Employer — Employee type of job is a fast food restaurant cashier. Let's say, you work the counter at *Bob's Burgers* taking order requests from customers. You have set work hours. Your boss has told you to come on Saturdays from 9 a.m. until 1 p.m. You cannot decide to come at 10 a.m. and stay until 2 p.m. because you have to follow the instructions of your employer.

You are the employee and your boss is the employer.

> **Employee:** The person with set work hours and a set job description.

> **Employer:** The person or company who sets the rules for what you will do, when you will do it, writes the paychecks, and at the end of the year, provides you with an IRS Form W-2 summarizing your pay for the year.

So, how do you find a job? You either hear about a job opening, someone recommends you to an employer, you see a *Help Wanted* sign, or maybe you look on the internet. Next, you apply for the job and hopefully you are accepted. The employer hires you. You may not be accepted the first time you try. This is very common and you should just try again. (That's what adults have to do too, so get used to being told, "No" and trying again.)

How do you tell someone you are the one to hire? You sell all the good qualities you have. When you speak to someone who will hopefully be your boss, you will want to tell them all the great things about yourself. This is not a time to be shy.

Here are some basic ideas to remember:

- Make eye contact with the person you are speaking to because this will show them you are confident
- Always firmly shake their hand which again displays confidence and maturity
- Dress neatly which shows you care about appearance.
- On an interview, have three questions in mind to ask about the job and if you can't think of any, try:
  o What happens if I am ill and cannot come to work?
  o Do you pay overtime?
  o Why did the last person leave the position?
  o Are there any benefits like store discounts or retirement plans included in the position?
- Tell your strengths with confidence. Here are ideas:
  o Highlight your good school attendance record as this shows you are reliable.
  o Explain the extracurricular activities you do which will show you understand teamwork, responsibility, and have an ability to get along with others.
  o Show any awards you have received which reveals that you will be a very hard worker.
  o Describe any classes you have taken, community service you do, or work experience you may have that will qualify you for the position you seek.

How much are you worth? How much should you be paid per hour? *Tax for Teens* reported ninety-one percent of high-school students made over minimum wage[4] so don't be shy to ask for decent pay. Ask around to see what the local rate is

---

[4] *Tax for Teens* by Stephen M. Rochford South-Western 2004

for children your age. The accepted rate will vary from state to state because some states are more expensive to live in than others. If you are more qualified than most children, you can and should charge a little more than the going rate.

Once someone decides to hire you, you will be asked to complete a *Form W-4, Employee's Withholding Allowance Certificate.* This form is required by law for anyone who is an employee. Some things may be confusing when you begin working but just take everything step by step.

The Form W-4 tells the employer how much to withhold from your pay for federal and state taxes. When you need to complete this form, take a look at the detailed chapter in this book that will help you, step by step. If you still have questions, you can ask your employer as well.

At the end of the year, usually by January 31, your employer, your boss, will give you a Form W-2.[5] This form will show all the money you have earned and any federal and state taxes that might have been withheld for that calendar year. The Form W-2 is a summary of your pay for the entire year including any deductions. (Like the Form W-4, we also have a detailed section on the Form W-2 later in this book to help with any questions you may have.)

Once you have your job, what is the next step to financial stability? First, we want to establish good employment records, good business records, which are important tools to help you plan what to do with your money. You should have good employment records for any type of job you have.

So how do we keep good business records? Let's make a work log called an *Income Sheet.* There is a full page of this sheet in the appendix in the back of this book. Let's look at how this sheet is set up.

---

[5] *IRS Instructions for Form W-2*

INCOME SHEET For: _____ (write your name and job here)

Date	Time In	Time Out	Task	Location	Hired By: Person & Phone	Amount paid

- **Date:** You enter the date you worked.
- **Time In:** You enter the time you arrived.
- **Time Out:** You enter the time you left.
- **Task Performed:** You enter the task (cashier, pizza delivery, etc.)
- **Location:** You enter where you worked (store, etc.)
- **Hired By:** You enter the name and phone of the person and company who hired you.
- **Amount Paid:** You enter the full amount paid. This is the amount of your take home paycheck. If you work 5 days a week and are paid every 2 weeks, then your amount paid would be $0 until your tenth day working.

This *Income Sheet* provides a nice reference of where you worked, for how long, and what you were paid. This also allows you to check that your employer did not forget any of your work hours. Everyone makes mistakes, even employers. If you receive a pay stub (a paper attached to your check summarizing pay and work hours) staple it to this sheet.

> Note: Jobs can include tip income. Waiters, hotel jobs, hair salon jobs, food delivery, cleaning, etc. can involve tips. If you receive tips over $20 in one month, you are required to report them to your employer who will include the amount in your wages at the end of the year.[6]

---

[6] Reporting Tips to Your Employer, *IRS Publication 531, Tip Income*

Let's look at an example:

Amy works at *Bob's Burgers* from 5 to 11 p.m. and she is paid every two weeks. After her first day, Amy's sheet would look like the one below. (After working 2 weeks, Amy would eventually have an amount in the paid column.)

INCOME SHEET For: _____ (write your name and job here)

Date	Time In	Time Out	Task	Location	Hired By: Person & Phone	Amount paid
5/7/ 2007	5 PM	11 PM	Cashier	Bob's B.	Bob Brown xxx-yyyy	$0

The next thing to do after you are employed is to open a savings account to deposit your paychecks. A good place to begin is with the bank your parents use. Inquire at their bank about how to open up a new account for a child. (Your parents may have to sign on the account with you depending on the bank.) Try to choose an account that has no fees and pays interest.

So, you have your job, you completed your Form W-4, and you opened your savings account to have somewhere to put each paycheck that is better than your piggy bank.

Time passes and your deposits are growing in your savings account. You say, "I'm going to go buy… (Insert something here that you just can't wait to purchase)."

But wait! What about *Good, Better, Best*? Before you spend any of your money, read the Roth IRA sections. Remember, you want to be like the educated farmer who starts early so your money has the longest time to grow. Put some of your money into a Roth IRA and let it grow tax free. (You should also read the tax chapter for this type of job.)

Job Type 1 Checklist Summary —
Working in an Employer — Employee Job

Kids:

- decide on the type of work you want
- apply for different jobs until you are hired
- each year, complete a Form W-4 (see later chapter)
- keep good work records, like an *Income Sheet*
- open a savings account
- read the Roth IRA sections of this book
- open a Roth IRA with a parent's assistance
- read the tax chapters, especially for Job Type 1, The Employer — Employee Job
- file your taxes each year

Parents:

- supervise and encourage all of the above as necessary
- assist your child in opening a savings account
- assist your child in opening a Roth IRA
- help your child complete his or her tax forms

Job Type 2: Employed in Your Parent's Business

If your mother or father owns their own business, you can work for them and gain some valuable work experience. Business types include sole proprietorships, partnerships, and various types of corporations. In a sole proprietorship or a partnership where the partners are only Mom and Dad,[7] unique tax benefits make payroll accounting fairly simple.

Can parents hire their kids?

In most cases, parents can hire their kids to work in the family business, regardless of the child's age. Check Federal Laws at **www.dol.gov** and a developing site for state laws at **www.youthrules.dol.gov/states.htm** (or use the home page **www.youthrules.dol.gov**).

First we need a job proposal for working in your parents business. It will include a description, work hours and wages.

Job Description: First you need to decide how you can help. What will your job be? Write a job description for yourself. The description can include multiple tasks such as filing, stuffing envelopes, washing the company car, labeling orders, downloading orders from the internet, counting inventory, and more. It should list all the tasks you think you could do to help in the family business. These should be necessary relevant tasks that your parents are currently accomplishing themselves or they might hire someone to do.

Work Hours: Add this to the job description as a separate section. When will you work and how often? Will you work only as needed? How will you keep track of your work hours? Will you use a time sheet?

---

[7] Family Employees, *IRS Publication 15, (Circular E) Employers Tax Guide*

Wages: How much will you be paid? Will it be an hourly wage or by the task completed? If you want to be paid because you are labeling products while watching your favorite TV show, then you probably need to be paid by the completed task and not by the hour.

Maybe some things will be paid by task and others paid by the hour. Also include in this section, how often you will be paid. Will it be monthly? Will it be weekly, quarterly or annually? Some businesses need to pay annually which is more like a bonus payment. For example, your parents could have a policy that all family members will be paid a bonus amount if the business reaches a certain goal. When deciding how much you should be paid, choose a wage amount comparable to what an outsider of your age would be paid.

With this information in hand, you will be able to ask your parents if you can work for them.

Will your parents hire you?

For your parent to hire you, their business must have the money to afford an employee. They must have the money to pay you. If for some reason, they cannot hire you, this is understandable and no different than if you walked into *Bob's Burgers* and the manager said, "I'm sorry, we are not hiring right now."

If your parents cannot hire you and you still want to start a Roth IRA, choose a different type of job (using another section in this book). There are many ways to obtain the earned income required for a Roth IRA.

At this point you should have your job description, which is really a job proposal for your parents to review. Well, if you work for your parent, your parent will be the employer and you will be the employee.

We are familiar with this:

Employee: has set work hours and a set job description.

Employer: sets the rules for what you will do and when you will do it, writes the paychecks, and provides a form W-2 summarizing your pay for the year.

Even though you came up with the idea of what work you can do, your parent is still the decision maker. Your parent is the boss who makes the decisions and thus the employer.

We already learned that when you are hired, you need to complete a Form W-4. It is no different when your parents hire you. So refer to the Form W-4 chapter of this book and complete a Form W-4. Give it to your parents to keep with their business records. (The law requires them to keep it.)

This book focuses on sole proprietorships and spouse partnership type businesses. Other family business types will need to obtain further guidance.

The next paragraphs will show how you can earn more money working for your parents because of special tax rules.

The following information is also important for parents because it shows the steps to hire you as an employee and the reasons why payroll for family employees is fairly simple in sole proprietorship or spouse partnership businesses.

The first step for parents employing family members is to obtain an Employer Identification Number (EIN) if they do not have one. This is a number that identifies the business. Parents can apply at **www.irs.gov/smallbiz** or by calling (800) 829-4933, *The Business & Specialty Tax Line*. Calling can be easier because all questions can be answered on the phone.

Employer Identification Number (EIN): An Employer Identification Number (EIN) is also known as a Federal Tax Identification Number, and is used to identify a business entity.

Because you are a family member, you are a family employee and you will qualify for special circumstances making things a lot easier for your self-employed parent. *IRS Publication 15 (Circular E) Employer's Tax Guide* states,

> *Child Employed by Parents:* "Payments for the services of a child under age 18 who works for his or her parent in a trade or business are not subject to Social Security and Medicare taxes if the trade or business is a sole proprietorship or a partnership in which each partner is a parent of the child."

And it further states:

> "Payments for the services of a child under age 21 who works for his or her parent, whether or not in a trade or business are not subject to the Federal Unemployment Tax Act (FUTA tax)."[8]

What does this all mean for your parents? They will be very pleased to not have to deal with Social Security, Medicare, and the Federal Unemployment Tax Act, FUTA taxes. This means hiring you to help out is much less paperwork than hiring your neighbor! This is a very good thing for them! And, this is a very good thing for you too. It means more money for you!

Let's look at Amy from the earlier section, who worked as a fast food cashier. When Amy worked 10 hours for $5 an hour, she did not take home $50 but instead took home a smaller check. This is because her employer withheld Social Security and Medicare taxes. They may have also withheld some federal and state income tax depending on what Amy asked for when she completed her W-4 for employment. The point is that Amy did not take home exactly $50.

---

[8] Family employees, Section 3, 2007 *IRS Publication 15 (Circular E) Employer's Tax Guide*

If you work 10 hours at $5 an hour for your parents, your check will be larger than Amy's because your parents do not have to withhold Social Security or Medicare tax. This is a good thing. In addition, if you claimed *Exempt* from income tax withholding when you completed your Form W-4 (see that chapter) your parents will not withhold federal taxes either. (Your parents will need to check on the requirements to withhold state taxes for your applicable state.) So, you can see that working for your parents gives you a larger paycheck because you save on Social Security and Medicare taxes! Your parents will like this too because there is no paperwork for them to report concerning Social Security and Medicare.

Parents who own their own business (even if it is not a sole proprietorship or spouse partnership type business) should definitely look for ways their children could assist. Hiring family members has more than one benefit. Besides the benefit of creating earned income for kids, parents will also be reducing their own taxes at the same time! How? Let's see. Since payroll is a deductible expense, employing children in the family business reduces net profit for the business. In some cases, parents may find the amount saved in taxes is equal to or more than what they paid their children!

Now, if you have approached your parents and they agreed to hire you and they obtained their EIN from the IRS, the next step is the same as with any job. You will open a savings account at a bank so you have somewhere to put your money where it earns interest.

Similarly, we also have a need for good record keeping. Your parents will definitely keep their own records of your work but I also recommend you keep track as well, just as described in the previous section. You can use the same *Income Sheet* described previously. Let's look at it again to see if there is anything that would be completed differently.

INCOME SHEET For: _____ (write your name and job here)

Date	Time In	Time Out	Task	Location	Hired By: Person & Phone	Amount paid

- **Date:** You enter the date you worked.
- **Time In:** You enter the time you began.
- **Time Out:** You enter the time you stopped working.
- **Task Performed:** You enter the task (filing, processing orders, taking inventory, internet work, whatever the task is).
- **Location:** You enter where you worked (home, fair, etc.)
- **Hired By:** You enter the name & phone of the business.
- **Amount Paid:** You enter the full amount paid, the amount your family gave you. Ask them to pay you by check, which is best for financial record keeping.

As you can see, not much is different. This is because in the last section and this section, we are just keeping track of what work you did, when you did it, and what you were paid. Keeping that in mind, the next paragraphs should also sound familiar.

Time passes and your deposits are growing in your savings account. You say, "I'm going to go buy… (Insert something here that you just can't wait to purchase)."

But wait! What about *Good, Better, Best*? Before you spend any of your money, read the Roth IRA sections. Remember, you want to be like the educated farmer who starts early so your money has the longest time to grow. Put some of your money into a Roth IRA and let it grow tax free. (You should also read the tax chapter for this type of job.)

Job Type 2 Checklist Summary —
To Work for a Self-Employed Parent:

Kids:

- write a job description for the type of work you can do
- each year, complete Form W-4 (see later chapter)
- keep good work records, like an *Income Sheet*
- open a savings account
- read the Roth IRA sections of this book
- open a Roth IRA with a parent's assistance
- read the tax chapters, especially for Job Type 2, Employed in Your Parents Business
- file your taxes each year

Parents:

- supervise and encourage all of the above as necessary
- obtain an EIN (Employee Identification Number)
- keep a Form W-4 on file
- keep records of child's work (dates, task, and payments)
- assist your child in opening a savings account
- assist your child in opening a Roth IRA
- each year, provide a Form W-2 by January 31st to child family employees (see the Form W-2 section) and by February 28th to the IRS[9]
- complete a Form W-4 for the next tax year
- help your child complete his or her tax forms

---

[9] When to File & Furnishing Copies, *IRS Instructions for Form W-2*

Job Type 3: Household Employee for Your Parents

Perhaps for some reason you are unable to obtain any of the jobs on the list. Maybe they don't interest you. Maybe you can't drive yet which eliminates some of the jobs. Maybe you are too young for many of the suggested jobs.

Well, you can always ask your mom or dad to hire you as their household employee. Now, they may not want to do this and they will have their reasons, but it is still worth looking into and asking. The worst situation would be that they say, "No."

You need to become used to hearing "No" anyway because it is normal to apply for many jobs and hear, "No" many times before you hear a "Yes. You're hired!" It is a good time to become accustomed to hearing an answer of "No" so you won't have hurt feelings when you apply for a job outside your family. Deal with it and move on. Explore some of the other job types in this book.

> ### Did you know?
>
> If you accomplish household tasks for someone who is not your parent, you are most likely considered "self-employed" as you are offering your services for pay and you will not receive a Form W-2. Refer to the self-employment sections for more information.

To approach your parents, we are going to use the same method we used in the last section where your parent was self-employed. We will write a full job description including work hours and wage proposal.

(Some of the text will even be exactly the same as the last chapter. This is because some readers of this book might only read by specific sections they are interested in, so some minimal repetition is useful.)

Job Description: First you need to decide how you can help. What will your job be? Write a job description for yourself. The description should be very detailed and include multiple tasks. These should be necessary and relevant tasks that typical household work would include. They might include some things people consider chores but you really want the job to be similar to what a cleaning lady would accomplish, similar to work your parents might hire someone to do in your home or out in the yard. Yes, yard work can count too.

> *Example*: Let's start with cleaning the bathroom. Take a sheet of paper and make a checklist of all the things that need to be accomplished to consider your bathroom cleaned. Write down cleaning the mirrors, cabinets (wipe down the outside), windows, sink, shower doors, tub, toilet (seat all the way to the floor), organize drawers, and mop the floor. And don't forget changing the towels! (See our appendix example.)

Other ideas of household work could include doing the laundry, cleaning the kitchen floor, stove top and burners, preparing dishes for the dish washer or washing them by hand, preparing meals, changing bed linens (remember to include parents' linens – just as a cleaning lady would), washing windows, dusting, and vacuuming. Household work can also include watering plants (inside and outside), raking leaves, and mowing the lawn.

Make the descriptions very detailed or in the form of a checklist so the actual work you are doing is very clear to someone who is not in your home.

Parents might think it sounds like you're asking to be paid for what they consider chores. It could be they already give you a weekly allowance for small tasks around the house. The job description needs to show them that it is actual work. It is not just a quick task such as taking the trash out to the curb. The description needs to convince the IRS too.

> **Household Employee:** "You have a household employee if you hired someone to do household work and that worker is your employee. The worker is your employee if you can control not only what work is done but how it is done..."

And the IRS further defines household work:

> **Household Work:** "Household work is work done in and around your home by the following people: Babysitters, Cleaning People, Housekeepers, Maids, Yard workers...."[10]

So if you are doing work *equivalent to hired help* and your parents are willing to pay you for it, you can be considered a household employee. Both you and your parents need to formalize things by documenting the work and wages paid.

Now, if your parents are not willing to pay you for the household work you do, that is their decision and it is final. It does not matter why they refuse to pay you. Maybe they think work builds good character or maybe they just don't have the cash. Don't fret. Go back to one of the other book sections and choose another path toward a Roth IRA.

But if you have your parent's approval, discuss wages with them.

Wages: How much will you be paid? Will it be an hourly wage or by the task completed? Also include in this section, how often you will be paid. Will it be monthly? Will it be weekly? Choose a wage amount comparable to what an outsider of your age would be paid or you can choose a lesser amount if the amount is acceptable to you.

Maybe you would accept only $2.00 a week if that is what your parents can afford. That is a good start. You might be

---

[10] Do You Have a Household Employee, *IRS Publication 926 Household Employers Guide*

thinking, "Cleaning that toilet is worth *way* more than $2.00 a week!" But if you save that $2.00, it will grow. The amount you accept depends on your personality, your generosity, and your view of the value of the work being accomplished.

What type of person are you? Do you walk by a penny on the ground or do you pick it up? What would happen if you picked up a million dollars in pennies? You would have a million dollars! No amount out. Actually, it is quite common for is too small when you are starting people to start at a low salary, learn and develop their skills, and then either promote to a higher paying job within the same company or move to a higher paying job at a different company. It is ok to start low.

Work Hours: Add this to the job description as a separate section. When will you work? Make it on a regular basis similar to that of hired help. How will you keep track of your hours? Will you use a time sheet? If you like to use computers, maybe you will use a spreadsheet.

Let's review. You work for your parent, your parent will be the employer and you will be the employee. We are familiar with this:

> **Employee:** has set work hours and a set job description.

> **Employer:** sets the rules for what you will do and when you will do it, writes the paychecks, and provides a form W-2 summarizing your pay for the year.

Even though you came up with the idea of what work you can do, your parent is still the decision maker. Your parent is the boss who makes the decisions and thus the employer.

We already learned that when you are hired, you need to complete a Form W-4. It is no different when your parents hire you. So refer to the Form W-4 chapter of this book and complete a Form W-4. Give it to your parents to keep with their business records. (The law requires them to keep it.)

The next paragraphs deal with information for both you and your parents. It is important for you because you will learn you can actually earn more money by working for your parents because of special rules. The following information is also important to your parents because they will learn the steps needed to make you an employee and understand the reasons why payroll is fairly simple for family employees.

The first step for parents employing family members is, to obtain an Employer Identification Number (EIN) if they do not have one. This is a number that identifies the business. Parents can apply at **www.irs.gov/smallbiz** or by calling (800) 829-4933, *The Business & Specialty Tax Line*. Calling can be easier because all questions can be answered on the phone.

> **Employer Identification Number (EIN):** An Employer Identification Number (EIN) is also known as a Federal Tax Identification Number, and is used to identify a business entity.

Because you are a family member, a family employee, you will qualify for special circumstances making things a lot easier for your parents. While this rule is very similar to the self-employed parent employing children, it is important to note that a different reference (*Household Employer Guide*) is used. This is where you will look to see if the law changes.

> "Wages not counted. Do not count wages you pay to any of the following individuals as Social Security or Medicare wages, even if these wages are $1,500 or more during the year {including} your child who is under age 21."[11]

What does this all mean for your parents? They will be very pleased to not have to deal with Social Security or Medicare withholding. The Federal Unemployment Tax Act, FUTA

---

[11] Social Security and Medicare Taxes, Wages not Counted, *IRS Publication 926 Household Employers Guide*

tax[12] rule from the last section also still applies so your parents will not have to deal with FUTA Taxes either.

This means hiring you to help out is much less paperwork than hiring your neighbor! This is a very good thing for them! And, this is a good thing for you too. It means more money!

Let's remember Amy from the earlier section, who worked as a fast food cashier. When Amy worked 10 hours for $5 an hour, she did not take home $50 but instead took home a smaller check. This is because her employer withheld Social Security and Medicare taxes. They may have also withheld some federal and state income tax depending on what Amy asked for when she completed her W-4 for employment. The point is that Amy did not take home exactly $50.

If you work 10 hours at $5 an hour for your parents, your check will be larger than Amy's because your parents do not have to withhold Social Security or Medicare tax. This is a good thing. In addition, if you claimed *Exempt* from income tax withholding when you completed your Form W-4 (see that chapter) your parents will not withhold federal taxes either. (Your parents will need to check on the requirements to withhold state taxes for your applicable state.) So you can see that working for your parents gives you a larger paycheck because you save on Social Security and Medicare taxes! Your parents will like this too because there is no paperwork for them to report concerning Social Security and Medicare.

When you have your parents' approval and they obtained their EIN, the next step is the same as in previous jobs. Open a savings account at a bank so your money will earn interest.

You also want to begin good record keeping. Similar to previous jobs, we also we have a need for good financial records. Your parents will definitely keep their own records

---

[12] Family employees, Section 3, 2007 *IRS Publication 15 (Circular E) Employer's Tax Guide*

of your work but you should keep track as well. Use the same *Income Sheet* described previously. Let's look to see if there is anything that would be completed differently.

INCOME SHEET For: _____ (write your name and job here)

Date	Time In	Time Out	Task	Location	Hired By: Person & Phone	Amount paid

- **Date:** You enter the date you worked.
- **Time In:** You enter the time you began.
- **Time Out:** You enter the time you stopped working.
- **Task Performed:** You enter the task. You might want to include an inspection checklist verified by your parent.
- **Location:** You enter where you worked (home or yard).
- **Hired By:** You enter the name of your parents.
- **Amount Paid:** You enter the full amount paid, the amount your parent gave you. Ask them to pay you by check, which is best for financial record keeping.

We are just keeping track of the type of work you did, when you did it, and what you were paid. So, if you read the prior sections, the next paragraphs will also sound familiar.

Time passes and your deposits are growing in your savings account. You say, "I'm going to go buy… (Insert something here that you just can't wait to purchase)."

But wait! What about *Good, Better, Best*? Before you spend any of your money, read the Roth IRA sections. Remember, you want to be like the educated farmer who starts early so your money has the longest time to grow. Put some of your money into a Roth IRA and let it grow tax free. (You should also read the tax chapter for this type of job.)

Job Type 3 Checklist Summary —
To work as household employees for your parents:

Kids:

- write a job description for the type of work you can do
- each year, complete Form W-4 (see later chapter)
- keep good work records, like an *Income Sheet*
- open a savings account
- read the Roth IRA sections of this book
- open a Roth IRA with a parent's assistance
- read the tax chapters, especially for Job Type 3, Household Employee for Parents
- file your taxes each year

Parents:

- supervise and encourage all of the above as necessary
- obtain an EIN (Employee Identification Number)
- keep a Form W-4 on file
- keep records of child's work (dates, task, and payments)
- assist your child in opening a savings account
- assist your child in opening a Roth IRA
- each year, provide a Form W-2 by January 31st to child family employees (see the Form W-2 section) and by February 28th to the IRS[13]
- complete a Form W-4 for the next tax year
- help your child complete his or her tax forms

---

[13] When to File & Furnishing Copies, *IRS Instructions for Form W-2*

Job Type 4: The Self-Employed Child

So you understand the Employer — Employee Relationship and you see how this is really the same relationship if your parents employ you, whether you work for your parents business or whether you work for them as their household employee. In all three cases you have a boss and you are the employee and you will receive a Form W-2.

You might begin thinking about employer responsibilities and ask, "But what if my employer is not going to provide a Form W-2?"

Well, if they are your employer, they must provide a Form W-2 for the work you have done. Let's review once again.

Employee: has set work hours and a set job description.

Employer: sets the rules for what you will do and when you will do it, writes the paychecks, and provides a form W-2 summarizing your pay for the year.

"But I am a babysitter. Other parents won't give me a Form W-2," you say in denial.

Yes, this is true. Parents who hire babysitters will not provide a Form W-2. Do you have a problem? Yes, but not with the parents. Your problem is in your thinking! You think the parent is your employer and the parent is not. The fact that the parents will not give you a Form W-2 breaks our definition itself and thus, they cannot be your employer.

The parents also fail our *setting the rules* test because they do not decide when you will work. They do not set your hours. They call you up and *you* decide if you would like to work at that time. You decide if you are available. It does not matter if you agree to baby-sit every Friday. You are still the one in control, the one setting the hours you will work.

"But they hired me! If they are not my employer, then who is?" you ask me.

The answer is you. You are your own employer! This is what we call self-employed. You are also what we call a sole proprietor.

> **Self-Employed:** a person who provides a product or service to others with the intention of making a profit.

> **Sole Proprietor:** someone who is in business for himself or herself and there is no other owner.

There is one exception to this idea that if you do not receive a Form W-2, you must be your own boss. The exception is if your income came from a hobby. Babysitting is not a very good example. Instead imagine you knitted a blanket and sold it to your neighbor and you do not intend to continue making blankets. This type of income would be considered *other income* from a hobby.

So when is income considered *other income* and when is income considered self-employment *business income*?

There are some guidelines to follow to ensure your income is business income and not hobby income. (You do not want your income to be considered other income from a hobby because it will not qualify as active earned income which is what you need for your Roth IRA contribution. Figuring out how to qualify for earned income is one of the main points in this book.)

The IRS provides guidelines to help you in determining if you activity is a hobby or business.[14] The key rule to justify your activity as a business is that you are actively trying to

---

[14] How do You Distinguish Between a Business and a Hobby
IRS Summertime Tax Tip 2007-13 at www.irs.gov

make a profit. You are actively engaged in this business activity for the sole purpose of making money.

This is not to say your business must be unpleasant. It is ok if you enjoy it as well. For example, if you love to cook and create a flyer so your neighbors can order cookies from you, this is still a business. It is reasonable to assume you are in this to make a profit and not baking 20 dozen cookies just because you love to cook.

You should try to run your activity in a business like fashion to prove you are trying to make a profit.

Things you can do to make your business look professional and help prove you are actively running your business in a businesslike manner are:

- Get a state license if required.
- Comply with local business laws.
- Advertise using flyers, business cards, or stationary
- Obtain a business website and business email address.
- Get a separate checking account for all business transactions. (Your parent may have to cosign depending on the bank. Keep a savings account for personal money.)
- Try not to have a business loss three years in a row (as this can be an indication you might not be trying hard enough to make a profit).

You also want to *materially participate* in your business. There are seven tests[15] for this and you only need to meet one. We will discuss two of the tests. The easiest test to meet is "Your participation in the activity for the tax year was substantially all of the participation in the activity of all

---

[15] Line G, Material Participation, *Schedule C Instructions*, at www.irs.gov

individuals." This means if you are running a dog walking business, you cannot have your little brother do all the work and then claim your activity is a business.

Another test you might qualify for is "You participated in the activity for more than 500 hours during the year." Thus, you should keep track of the time you spend working which is why this book recommends and gives you the tools to have good records.

You only need to meet *one* of the seven tests and those two tests should work for most kids receiving earned income.

Which jobs are self-employment jobs? Let's review our list of possible employment for kids. Take a pencil and place a check next to each job that would be self-employment.

- acting
- artist
- babysitter
- cashier
- camp counselor
- cook
- dog walker
- elderly assistant
- filing
- gardening
- grocery bagging
- household cleaning
- lawn mowing
- lemonade stand
- modeling
- moving assistant
- musician
- newspaper delivery
- office assistant
- party assistant
- painter
- pet-sitter
- pizza delivery
- plant sitter
- raking leaves
- recycling assistant
- restaurant bus boy
- selling baked goods
- selling craft items
- street entertainer (singing, break dancing, clown, etc.)
- stuffing envelopes
- ticket taker (movie, museum, etc.)
- tutoring
- waitress
- water gardens
- writer - traditional
- writer - self-publisher
- window cleaner

Are there some that could be either Employer — Employee or self-employment? Yes, there are!

A lawn mower company might hire you to work with them for the summer, but you could also post a flyer in the neighborhood asking neighbors to call you to mow their lawn for $40. In the first idea, someone hired you, thus creating an Employer — Employee relationship. In the second idea, you are the boss and thus, considered self-employed.

When you are thinking of going into business for yourself, think about:

- choosing something you like so it will be fun
- your talents and strengths
- your personality
  - o whether you like working alone or with others
  - o where you like to work (outside or indoors)
  - o whether you like talking with people (Do you like to speak to customers? Are you shy?)
- how much time you have to work
- what you will need for supplies
- what price you might charge
- a need in your neighborhood that your job could solve
- considering the competition (if someone else already does the job)

Read for ideas!

Two fun books about self-employment are *In Business with Mallory* by Laurie Friedman and *Lawn Boy* by Gary Paulsen. If your parents let you watch the hit series, *The Apprentice*, you may also enjoy *Beyond the Lemonade Stand* by *Apprentice* winner, Bill Rancic. See more book ideas in the appendix.

When I first approached my daughter about Roth IRAs and self-employment, she was far from pleased.

"Mom, no babysitter pays taxes! I'm not giving my money to the IRS! Get real!" my eleven year old told me.

Well, I can't find anything that says student babysitters are excused from paying taxes. On the other hand, on the IRS website, run a search for "student" and an article discussing taxable income for students, does say:

"Earnings you received from self-employment are subject to income tax. These earnings include income from babysitting and lawn mowing. These services are not self-employment if you provided these services as an employee."[16]

Well, we have learned you are only an employee if you have an employer and I would refer you to a few paragraphs back where we discussed the fact that most parents will not be providing Form W-2's to babysitters. (Some parents might provide a Form W-2 if you are a regular household nanny.)

Stick with the law. Check that the law is the same each year and always comply. Besides, you want your babysitting money to be taxable, to be active earned income, so you can qualify for contributions to your Roth IRA and let your money grow tax free! So this is actually a good thing.

Here is one more IRS reference for those of you who are babysitters, one of the most popular jobs for kids. Let's look at some statements from IRS publications:

Babysitting: "If you baby-sit for relatives or neighborhood children, whether on a regular basis or only periodically, the rules of childcare providers apply to you."[17]

---

[16] Taxable income for students
www.irs.gov/individuals/students/article/0,,id=96674,00.html
[17] *IRS Publication 525, Taxable and Nontaxable Income*

And when you read the rules for childcare providers,

Childcare Providers: "If you provide child care, either in the child's home or in your home or other place of business, the pay you receive must be included in your income. If you are not an employee, you are probably self-employed and must include payments on Schedule C." [18] (Schedule C is a tax form we will discuss later.)

So for my daughter and all the other youths babysitting, there it is. Babysitting money must be included in your taxable income! By law babysitting money is taxable.

Did you know?

While babysitting money does count as taxable income, you would have had to earn more than $5,350 as your annual income in 2007 to actually pay federal taxes. However, if your net income was over $400, you still *must file* a tax return to pay your self-employment taxes.

Don't panic. You are not going to jail. There is a reason most young babysitters do not pay taxes. The IRS rules allow for certain deductions which reduce a person's taxable income. When babysitters reduce their taxable income salary by the amount of these deductions, often there is no taxable income left.

To owe federal taxes on your babysitting money in 2007, you would have had to earn over $5,350! However, even if you earned less than $5,350, if your *net earnings* were more than $400, you must file a tax return to pay self-employment tax.[19] (We will discuss this more in the sections on taxes.)

---

[18] *IRS Publication 525, Taxable and Nontaxable Income*
[19] Do I have to file a tax return? *IRS Publication 334, Tax Guide for Small Business*

One nice thing about being in business for yourself is the child labor laws will not apply to you. You are never too young to work for yourself. If your parents would not hire you or you are having trouble finding a local job because, for example, you are too young to bag groceries, then maybe starting your own business is the answer for you.

Because no one is going to provide you with a Form W-2, and you are engaged in your activity for the purpose of making a profit, we have established that your work, your job, whatever it is, babysitting, lawn mowing, dog walking, etc., qualifies as self-employment.

Let's look at what this means. What will be different for you than what we covered in the previous sections?

This is going to be a little uncomfortable. You may think, "Forget it. I don't want to do it. I've changed my mind. I don't want to have this tax-free wealth account after all."

You may have that awful feeling that comes in Science class when they explain for the next assignment you have to invent something for the Science Fair. That feeling can be described as, "Ugh! Where do we start? I don't want to do this... It's too difficult!" But it is not too difficult. It is just uncomfortable because it is unfamiliar.

Let's look at self-employment step by step. First, you will need to research if your state requires a business license. Usually the easiest way to check this is to go to the internet. (Use a library computer if you do not have one.) A librarian may be able to assist you. On the internet, visit the search engine:

www.google.com

In the search box, using quotes, enter your state and the words business license as in: "(your state) business license." Usually one of the top 5 websites will have the rules for your state. Look for an internet website address like this www.state.(state abbreviation goes here).us where your state abbreviation in the parenthesis (but the parenthesis are not used). Here are some examples to illustrate what the internet address might look like:

- www.state.fl.us is the address for Florida information
- www.state.in.us is the address for Indiana information
- www.state.tx.us is the address for Texas information

You may try other sites that were in the search results as well because sometimes they rephrase a law making it easier to understand. Each state website will be different with different links and state rules so this book does not go into more details but instead gives you the location to research more on what is applicable to your state.

You want to research until you have something *in writing* that says you do need a license or something that proves you do not need a license. An example of something that proves you do not need a license would be information printed off the internet that states a license is only required if (insert some rules here) and your job does not fall under those rules. Keep this license information with your work records.

While you are doing this research, you also want to search the internet for whom to ask about guidance for *state sales tax*. This applies to those of you who will be selling a product. For example, if you are going to sell craft items, you may need to charge sales tax on the items when you sell them. If you sell lemonade, since it is food, usually there is no sales tax. After collecting the sales tax, you would send this collected tax to your state. Ask questions and have paperwork sent to you to explain how to handle sales tax in your business. (Just take it one step at a time. Remember it is only unfamiliar, not difficult.) Sales tax is also unique to each state so I cannot provide the specific answers for you here.

If you do need a license, some states will have a fee for this, usually from $10 to $50 and it may be a one-time fee or a fee you have to renew each year. This is called *start up money*.

> **Start up money – Start up costs:** Money you spend on your business before you sell products or provide your actual service. Money spent to start your business.

Where are you going to get that money from?

If you have a weekly allowance, you can use that. If Grandma or Aunt Sophie gave you birthday money, you can use that. If you are not paid an allowance and never received money as a gift, then you will have to take a loan. Loans are very common in business. In fact, loans are the way most businesses have to start. Almost every business creates a business plan and approaches banks or family for a loan to get started. So, be comfortable in requesting a loan from your parents if you need it.

To request a loan, write down your plan, how much you need and when you intend to pay it back. (This is the same procedure followed by new businesses approaching a bank.)

> *Example:* Mary wrote down, "I plan to baby-sit occasionally over the next few years. One of my goals is to contribute to a Roth IRA. My job is considered self-employment by the IRS. I contacted our state department and found out I need $25 for a business license. I would like to borrow it from Mom and will pay it back within a year with no interest." (Yes, always ask for no interest!)

So, this book is going to assume Mom said, "Yes" and Mary purchased her license and now Mary is legally a self-employed babysitter. Good job Mary! What happens next?

Mary opens a savings account so she can earn interest. This is similar to all the other job types we discussed.

Mary should also open a checking account (with her parents help) to be used only for business. This way if she needs to purchase supplies at a store, she can write a check or use a debit card that will come with the checking account.

Mary's employment will be very similar to someone who worked as an employee as a fast food cashier. The cashier provided a service of assisting customers. Mary is providing a service of assisting parents. She goes to work and she gets paid (but she probably receives cash). She deposits all her business cash into her checking account.

Remember we had the fast food cashier keep good business records? Well, Mary needs to keep good business records too. But hers are a little different. Mary will use two records for her business. Like the other jobs, she will have an *Income Sheet*, but she will also keep track of her business expenses, using an *Expense Sheet*. Let's look at these sheets. Remember the *Income Sheet* looks like this:

INCOME SHEET For: _____ (write your name and job here)

Date	Time In	Time Out	Task	Location	Hired By: Person & Phone	Amount paid

- **Date:** Mary enters the date she worked.
- **Time In:** Mary enters the time she arrived.
- **Time Out:** Mary enters the time she left.
- **Task Performed:** Mary enters the task (babysitting).
- **Location:** Mary enters where she worked (home, park, zoo, etc.)
- **Hired By:** Mary enters the name and phone of the person who hired her.
- **Amount Paid:** Mary enters the full amount paid.

Well, that is very similar to the Employer — Employee job relationship in the previous section. She is just logging in the work completed and how much she was paid.

But Mary is self-employed so she can also have business expenses. Mary's first expense is her license fee. (Remember she borrowed money for her business license?) Her sheet would look like:

EXPENSE SHEET – Staple Receipts to the back

Date Incurred	Date Paid	Expense Amount	Expense Description	Expense Category
5/5/07	5/5/07	$25	Business License	License fee

- **Date Incurred:** Mary enters the date the expense occurred.
- **Date Paid:** Mary enters the date she actually paid the expense.
- **Amount Paid:** Mary enters the amount she spent.
- **Expense Description:** Mary enters a short description of why she spent the money.
- **Expense Category:** Mary will learn about categories such as advertising or supplies and this is the entry she will write in this column.

If Mary was unsure of the category, it would be fine to leave that column blank until tax time when she would research or ask for help with determining the category. (All expenses are grouped into different categories for taxes.)

All business expenses must be ordinary (common and accepted) and necessary (appropriate and helpful).

This means Mary cannot go out a buy an expensive leather jacket (claiming it was cold when she babysat children in the park) and call it a business expense. A reasonable person would not consider that expense ordinary and necessary.

However, Mary might arrive at every babysitting job with a basket of comic books that she shares with children she cares for. She takes the comic books home with her so she can use them for every job. Parents like that she encourages reading and this makes her unique from other babysitters.

The comic books are necessary (appropriate and helpful) to give her a unique trait and they are ordinary in the sense that it is logical and acceptable that Mary would bring something for the children to read. The comic books would count as a business expense under the supply category.

What if Mary was selling a product? How would she record items sold? She can use the *Sales Sheet* in the appendix. Let's look at how the *Sales Sheet* is set up.

SALES SHEET For Self-Employed

Date	Item Sold	# Sold	Total Received	Cost of Goods Sold	Profit

- **Date:** Mary enters the date she made the sale.
- **Item Sold:** Mary enters the item sold.
- **# Sold:** Mary enters the quantity of the item sold.
- **Total Received:** Mary enters the total of the sale.
- **Cost of Goods Sold:** Mary enters the cost of the items, how much she paid for them.
- **Profit:** Mary will subtract the Cost of Goods Sold (CGS) from the total received to compute her profit.

If Mary is crafting items using a mixture of materials, she will need a way to determine the cost of each crafted item sold. If needed, Mary should consult a tax professional to help her with the *Cost of Goods Sold* as every case is unique. (We will touch on this idea a little more in our tax example where products are sold.)

Let's come back to you. You determined you have a self-employment type of job. You researched about the need for a business license and purchased one if it was necessary. You set yourself up to have good financial records by copying the income, sales, and expense sheets in the appendix of this book. Next, you open a checking account for business money you receive and a savings account for personal money to earn interest.

Business funds must be kept separate from personal funds. To earn interest on your money or to use some of your profit for personal use, after depositing business funds into your checking account, make a withdrawal from the checking account and either spend it or deposit the amount into your savings account. This can be referred to as an *owners draw*. You own the business and withdrew money for personal use.

Wow! We are doing great. Time passes. You are working hard and you are depositing your pay.

If you have read the previous sections, the following should sound very familiar. Time has passed and your deposits are growing in your account. You say, "I'm going to go buy… (Insert something here that you just can't wait to purchase)."

But wait! What about *Good, Better, Best*? Before you spend any of your money, read the Roth IRA sections. Remember, you want to be like the educated farmer who starts early so your money has the longest time to grow. Put some of your money into a Roth IRA and let it grow tax free. (You should also read the tax chapter for this type of job.)

Job Type 4 Checklist Summary — Working as a Self-Employed Person:

Kids:

- decide on the type of work you want to do
- research state laws on the need for a business license
- research state sales tax if you are selling a product
- keep good work records, like the *Income Sheet*, *Sales Sheet*, and *Expense Sheet*
- open a savings account (personal)
- open a checking account (to be used for business)
- read the Roth IRA sections of this book
- open a Roth IRA with a parent's assistance
- read the tax chapters, especially those for Job Type 4, Self-Employed Child
- file your taxes each year

Parents:

- supervise and encourage all of the above as necessary
- help with business license cost, if needed
- help with sales tax, if needed
- assist your child in opening a savings account
- assist your child in opening a checking account
- assist your child in opening a Roth IRA
- help your child complete his or her tax forms

Roth IRA Issues

The Time Value of Money

Now that you know many options to meet the Roth IRA requirement to have earned income, it is time to look more at the Roth IRA itself. The earlier you begin to contribute your earned money in your Roth IRA, the more money you will have at retirement age.

Why should you be concerned with retirement at a young age? First, if you do not have any money saved at retirement, you may have little more than Social Security to support yourself.

> **Did you know?**
>
> Many jobs do not offer any type of retirement plan. Workers with no retirement plan will have to rely on Social Security to support them at retirement age unless they have alternative funds saved on their own. One way to save is a Roth IRA.

Another reason is you want to take advantage of what we call the *time value of money*. This idea means the sooner you save, the more time you will dedicate towards compounding interest. There is more time for your money to grow.

What if you are 16 years old? Is it too late? Should you bother? How has the lost time affected you? Can you catch up to your friend who started contributing at age 8?

Let's look at *The Tale of Two Savers*. This is a common example given in financial magazines and you can also find a mixture of versions of the story on the internet. (Search using quotations marks around the words as in: *"Tale of Two Savers."*) The names and figures will vary in each story but the message is the same, to learn about *the time value of money*.

The figures in this book are from a Fidelity Investment brochure[20] which used an 8% annual return. To understand the chart, we've made up a story:

> Jean began investing at age 21 by contributing $1,000 to a Roth IRA every year. At the same time, she convinced her brother, Rob, who was 35 years old to also begin investing $1,000 in his Roth IRA. Jean stopped contributing after 10 years when she became disabled, stopped working and had no earned income. *But her account kept growing because of compounding earnings.* Rob continued to contribute for a total of 30 years, all the way until he retired. The chart shows the potential value of both of their IRAs at age 65.

	Started IRA at Age	Stopped Contributions At Age	Total Contributed	Years Contributed	Potential value at age 65
Jean	21	30	$ 10,000	10	$214,189
Rob	35	64	$ 30,000	30	$122,346

- How much did Jean contribute over her life? $10,000
- How much did Rob contribute over his life? $30,000
- Who had more money in the end? Jean, with $214,189, has $91,843 more than Rob!

Rob never caught up with Jean even though he contributed $20,000 more! This is because Jean began early! Over time, compounding earnings (money earned on money) made the major difference between the values of the accounts.

So, back to the original question, is 16 years old too late? No, of course not! It is never too late. If you start your IRA at age 16, that is better than starting at age 17. If you start your IRA at age 45, that is better than starting at age 46. The idea is to start now, once you understand the *time value of money.*

---

[20] Overcoming the Excuses... *Fidelity Investment Brochure,* www.urs.org/general/pdf/brochures/ira_guidebook.pdf

The Value of a Tax-Free Account

Let's take an even closer look at the Roth IRA. We learned previously, in many ways, a Roth IRA is just another type of savings account similar to your bank savings account. One big difference is the Roth IRA grows tax free.

We learned that the Roth IRA was the *Best* in our choices of *Good, Better, Best*. When you put money in a piggy bank at home, you made the first step, the *Good* step toward saving. When you decided to deposit your piggy bank money into your savings account, you made the *Better* step.

When you decide to deposit your savings account money into a Roth IRA, you have made the *Best* step. You have chosen an account that grows tax free. This means you do not have to pay taxes on the money the account earns.

You will recall, when you earn interest in your bank savings account, you are required to report this on your income tax form and pay taxes on it. In other words, the government is going to take some of that interest you earned.

In a Roth IRA, the government will not take any of your earnings if you follow the rules.

To see the tax saving benefits of choosing a Roth IRA, you can search using quotes for "Roth IRA calculator" at:

www.Google.com

Of the results, the calculator I liked best was:

www.dinkytown.net/java/RothIRA.html

However, you can most likely use any calculator that showed in your results. The reason I liked this particular calculator is it compares the growth of a Roth IRA with that of a taxable savings account. Also, below the calculator chart, there are definitions explaining each term, so you can understand what you are reading.

To use this calculator, you will enter a starting balance, current age, expected rate of return, annual contribution, retirement age, and tax rate.

Let's demonstrate using the calculator. Enter 0 for starting balance, 16 for current age, 5% for expected rate of return, $80 for annual contribution, 65 for a retirement age, and 15% for the tax rate. Then click on the *calculate* button. The results show if a 16 year old contributes only $80 a year and *continues to contribute only $80 every year* to a Roth IRA, the Roth IRA would grow tax free to $16,668 at retirement. (This number is next to the graph.) If the same money had been put into a taxable savings account, it would have only grown to $13,121! The Roth IRA has $3,547 more because of the tax-free savings!

The three factors that make the big difference in the final balance of your Roth IRA at retirement are:

- the amount contributed
- the tax-free compounding growth
- the *time value of money*

The *amount* of money contributed makes a big difference. Let's change the amount for the 16 year old by increasing it from $80 each year to $500 each year (which might be a typical salary for a part time summer job). This time the Roth IRA for the 16 year old grows to $104,174. That is $87,506 more than when only $80 was contributed each year! This happened because each year more money was contributed which resulted in even more compounded earnings.

The 16 year old also has the *tax-free compounding growth* benefits. If this same 16 year old had left the money in a typical taxable savings account in a bank, that account would only have grown to $82,008. Again, we see tax-free savings are important. By contributing to a tax-free Roth IRA, this 16 year old earned $22,166 more! ($104,174 - $82,008 = $22,166.)

Our chart shows a comparison of a taxable account with a tax-free account,illustrating the value of tax-free growth.

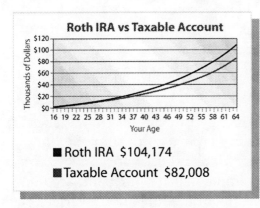

Roth IRA vs Taxable Account

■ Roth IRA $104,174

■ Taxable Account $82,008

Tax Free Roth IRA Investment Example:

– Age 16
– Contributes $500 per year
– Return of 5%
– Tax Bracket of 15%

= $104,174 at age 65!

$22,166 more than in a taxable investment account

Let's look at the *time value of money* again. What would happen if an 8 year old did the same as our 16 year old? (Remember the 8 year old is starting earlier so he has more time for his money to grow.) Change only one entry from our previous example. Change the age from 16 to 8 and leave a 0 starting balance, 5% return rate, $500 contribution, 65 for the retirement age, and a 15% tax rate.

At retirement age, the 8 year old has $158,926! Remember the 16 year old had $104,174, so the eight year old has $54,752 more at retirement age. Again, just like *The Tale of Two Savers*, we see the difference time makes!

Play with the calculator. Change other factors like the rate of return to see how your money would grow if the rate was higher. (Often Roth IRAs earn 8% or more. Our examples used 5% as a reasonable conservative guaranteed amount.)

The calculator can be fun and motivating! Hopefully it will make you want to get started on a Roth IRA now.

Remember, if you are a minor you will need your parent's help to open a Roth IRA account. Your parent will sign as the custodian of the account, but all the money belongs to you. (At age 18, you can open a Roth IRA on your own.)

What is your Comfort Zone?

IRAs are financial investment accounts. Let's look at what happens to money when it is in an IRA. Money deposited into an IRA is called a contribution.

> **IRA Contribution**: the amount of earned income that one contributes or deposits into an IRA.

When you deposit your money into an IRA, the financial organization gives you earnings (pays you a sum of money) because you are letting them hold and use your money. You learned about something similar when your bank account paid you interest. IRA investment accounts use a variety of names for the earnings: interest, dividends, or capital gains.

When you put your money into a Roth IRA, it is in a financial investment account set up through a bank, a mutual fund company, or a brokerage firm. Your parents (along with the bank, mutual fund company, or brokerage firm) will help you decide *what type of investment* to contribute your money to. The Roth IRA is only the type of account. You need to go a step further and decide what type of investment to purchase.

Just like money comes in the form of pennies, nickels, dimes, quarters, and dollar bills, there are several types of Roth IRAs that can be set up. They are all called Roth IRAs.

- *Money Market Accounts:* Your IRA earns interest or dividends, similar to a bank savings account.
- *Stocks:* Your IRA consists of something called *shares*. Shares are a tiny piece of ownership in a company. When the company is successful you are rewarded by the value of your shares increasing and/or receiving dividends or capital gains (which are like interest).
- *Mutual Funds:* Your IRA is invested similar to stocks but each share you own represents ownership in a mixture of companies. The account is more diverse.

Another way to understand would be to think of your Roth IRA account as a market or a toy store. Even though you have decided to invest your money in the store, you still have to decide if you money will be represented in the doll aisle, the bike aisle, the cell phone aisle, or some other aisle. Your investment will own a little piece of the market or store.

Your final decision depends on your comfort zone.

Comfort Zone: How one feels about investing his or her money when taking into account risk and expected performance of the investment.

This means your emotions will play a role in your money making decisions. Do you want a safe and steady investment? Do you want an investment that could grow extremely fast but also has the risk that you could lose your money?

Personality Plays a Role

Personality plays a role in finances. Which of these would be a good financial decision?
- Buy a lottery ticket
- Recycle (reuse) wrapping paper or decorative bag from a gift you received
- Wash out a plastic baggie and let it dry so you can reuse it
- Reuse last year's crayons and pencils for school instead of buying new ones

In the store example, you may think your money should be in the cell phone aisle because cell phones are popular, so the store will sell a lot of them each month which means your money will grow very fast. But there is risk involved because if an electronics store creates a better cell phone, customers will go to the electronics store instead of the toy store. If your phones sit on the store shelf, your money will not grow.

There is a risk factor involved. Considering the *risk* of the phones becoming unpopular, you might choose as an alternative, to put your money in the doll aisle. Since little girls are born everyday and they usually love dolls, chances are the dolls will continuously sell at a steady pace. No one will be lining up outside the store waiting to purchase the dolls, but at the same time, you don't have to worry that the dolls might become unpopular. The dolls will sell at a steady pace and your money will grow at a steady rate.

Everyone has his or her own comfort zone for money. There is no such thing as a right or wrong comfort zone. Your comfort zone along with the *time value of money* and value of tax-free growth will help you make your final decision. Your parents along with advisors from the bank, mutual fund company, or brokerage firm, will help you find the best type of investment security for positive growth in your IRA.

Once you have a steady job, it is a good idea to follow the practice of *Dollar Cost Averaging*.

> **Dollar Cost Averaging:** Investing the same amount in the same investment on a regular basis for a long period of time resulting in the purchase of more shares when the price is low and fewer shares when the price is high.

Dollar Cost Averaging works well if you can invest a set amount on a monthly basis with no fees applied. Dollar Cost Averaging means: investing $25 a month for 12 months is better than investing $300 ($25 x 12 months) all at one time.

Since share prices fluctuate, by investing the exact same amount, you will buy more shares when the price is low and fewer shares when the price is high. This will result in reaching the goal of an account of higher value because your purchases are spread over different cost amounts. Learn more about investing from *Street Wise: A Guide for Teen Investors* by Janet Bamford or the other resources in the appendix.

IRA Rules and Limits

There are actually two types of IRAs: a Roth IRA and a Traditional IRA. We recommend you open up a Roth IRA.

Let's see why the Roth IRA is recommended for you. A full page summary chart is shown later to use as a quick reference for comparison of the Roth and the Traditional IRA. We will explain similarities and differences by looking at the chart in sections. The first three items are the same for both:

ROTH IRA	TRADITIONAL IRA	Comparison
No age limit to begin contributing.	No age limit to begin contributing.	Same rule for both.
Must have earned income.	Must have earned income.	Same rule for both.
Limited amount may be contributed each year (check with the IRS) and an April 15th deadline for contributing.	Limited amount may be contributed each year (check with the IRS) and there is an April 15th deadline for contributing.	Same rule for both.

First, you can start at any age. (Even a baby model working for a magazine can contribute to an IRA.)

Second, you must have earned income (which means allowance and birthday gifts do not count).

Third, both types have a contribution limit each year along with a contribution deadline which is the due date of your tax return (usually April 15th). What is a contribution limit?

> **IRA Contribution Limit:** is the maximum amount allowed by the IRS for the applicable year or the amount of your earned income, whichever amount is *less*. [21]

---

[21] *IRS Publication 590, Individual Retirement Arrangements*

The first part means the IRS sets a maximum contribution amount each tax year. You cannot contribute more than this amount. The amount changes so be sure to check with the IRS every year. For 2006 and 2007, $4,000 was the maximum contribution amount allowed for children. In 2008, the maximum is $5,000. This means, even if you earn $8,000 for modeling in 2008, you can only contribute up to $5,000.

The second part of the limit rule says you cannot contribute more than your earned income (if it is less than the maximum contribution limit). This means, in 2008, if you earn $2,000, you can choose to contribute anywhere from $1 up to $2,000 (your earned income) but nothing higher than $2,000.

The contribution limits apply to your income for that particular year. You cannot combine income that was earned in different years. If you ever discover that you have *excess contributions* (you have contributed too much to your IRA), immediately consult with a tax professional.

The first chart difference concerns deducting contributions:

ROTH IRA	TRADITIONAL IRA	Comparison
You cannot deduct contributions from taxable income.	You may be able to deduct contributions from taxable income.	**Different rules.**

Roth IRA contributions *cannot* be deducted from taxable income and Traditional IRA contributions can.

What does this mean? Remember when you earn money, you pay taxes based on your taxable income. If in 2007, Katie earns $6,000 and Bill earns $5,000, then we expect Katie will pay more taxes than Bill because she earned more.

Traditional IRA amounts can be deducted to reduce taxable income. If Katie contributes $4,000 to a Traditional IRA, she is allowed to deduct $4,000 from her total income. Now Katie will only be taxed on $2,000. (Katie's earned income of $6,000 minus her $4,000 Traditional IRA contribution = $2,000.)

That sounds great, right? Well, not exactly. To understand why, let's look at the next section of the chart.

ROTH IRA	TRADITIONAL IRA	Comparison
Your money (contributions and earnings) will grow tax-free.	Your money grows tax deferred. You pay taxes on withdrawals of both earnings and contributions.	**Different rules.**

Katie's money, in a Traditional IRA, grows *tax deferred*.

Tax Deferred: means taxes are postponed. Taxes are not paid today but will be paid at a later date.

Katie still owes the taxes on the $4,000. She will have to pay the taxes on that $4,000 when she withdraws the money out of her Traditional IRA. (Katie also pays taxes later on her earnings!) So all she has done is *delay* the payment of taxes.

If Katie chooses to contribute $4,000 to a Roth IRA instead, she will report her taxable income as $6,000. However, Katie can still reduce her income by subtracting out her *Standard Deduction* ($5,350 for 2007) which will reduce her taxable income enough so she will pay little or no tax anyway! (Standard deduction is discussed more in the tax sections.)

Standard Deduction: a dollar amount you may subtract from your taxable income based upon filing status.

Katie's Traditional Choice	Katie's Roth Choice
$ 6,000 earned income -$4,000 (deferred Traditional Contribution) = $2,000 Adjusted Taxable income -$5,350 Standard Deduction = 0 taxable income for 2007	$ 6,000 earned income (no deduction allowed for $4,000 Roth Contribution) -$5,350 Standard Deduction = $ 650 taxable income for 2007
Katie still owes tax on $4,000 later.	Katie owes no tax later.
Total income taxed: $4,000	Total income taxed: $650

The next chart comparison deals with withdrawals:

ROTH IRA	TRADITIONAL IRA	Comparison
You can withdraw your *contribution* amount at any time without penalty and without having to pay tax on it.	You pay both a penalty and taxes for withdrawing your contribution amount before age 59½. After age 59½ you pay taxes but no penalty.	**Different rules**

This book recommends no withdrawals before retirement, but you should still understand the rules. If you have a Roth IRA, you can withdraw your contribution amount at any time without penalty or taxes due. This rule only applies to the Roth IRA and only applies to contributions, *not earnings*.

> **IRA Contribution**: is the amount of earned income that one contributes to a Roth IRA. Contributions can be made from January 1 through the date taxes are due the following year.

> **IRA Earnings:** is the amount of money in your IRA that exceeds your contributions.

If Katie contributes to a Traditional IRA and chooses to take some money out before age 59½, she will pay a penalty and owe taxes on her withdrawal. By contributing to a Roth IRA she will have flexibility. She has the option to withdraw contributions at any time with no penalty or taxes due.

Remember, a Roth IRA has both *contributions* and *earnings* and each is treated differently.

Earnings in a Roth IRA account cannot be withdrawn before age 59½ without paying taxes and penalties on them. (There are a few exceptions to this, like disability and first time home purchases.)[22]

You must keep good records so you know how much of your total balance is contributions and how much of your total balance is earnings. The appendix provides a sheet.

ROTH IRA CONTRIBUTION SHEET

Date	Contribution for Year	Amount Contributed	Amount Allowed	Account Value on Dec 31

Use this sheet to run a total of all the money contributed. Subtract this from your account value, to get your earnings. Let's see how this sheet works by using an example.

Example: Maria worked bagging groceries and earned $300 for 2006 and $300 for 2007. Maria could contribute between $1 and $300 each year. She was allowed to contribute up to her earned income or $4,000, whichever was *less*. Maria contributed all her paychecks into her Roth IRA. Maria's statement for her Roth IRA shows she has a $650 balance on Dec. 31, 2007.

On Maria's completed sheet, her total balance is $650. She subtracts her contributions of $600 ($300 received each year) which results in $50 which is her earnings amount.

ROTH IRA CONTRIBUTION SHEET

Date	Contribution for Year	Amount Contributed	Amount Allowed	Account Value on Dec 31
10/1/2006	2006	300	4000	335
11/1/2007	2007	300	4000	650

---

[22] What are qualified distributions in *IRS Publication 590, Individual Retirement Arrangements*

The last difference is Required Mandatory Distributions:

ROTH IRA	TRADITIONAL IRA	Comparison
No mandatory distributions. Earnings must be left 5 yrs *and* until age 59½ (unless an exception is met).	Required Mandatory Distributions (RMDs) begin annually before April 1 of the year following the year you turn age 70½.	**Different rules**

> **Required Mandatory Distributions (RMDs):** A minimum amount of money you are required to withdraw annually beginning no later than April 1 of the year following the year you turn age 70½.

A Roth IRA has no Required Mandatory Distributions (unless inherited, which we discuss later in the chapter on the IRA Gift). A Traditional IRA does. This is one more advantage of the Roth IRA. You never have to take the money out.

Why is this important? If you do not need your money at retirement and it is in a Roth IRA, it continues to grow tax free. If you have a Traditional IRA, once you turn age 70½, you have to take some money out on an annual basis.

The freedom to leave your money in an account and let it grow as long as possible is very valuable. After all, we have emphasized the *time value of money.* If your money is in a Traditional IRA, someone else decides when you have to take it out. You have lost some of your freedom, lost some of your power to make your money grow.

How would you like if I came to you and said, "Hey that's great that you saved all your paychecks! Now, I want you to withdraw $10 every month."

Well, what does that mean for you? If you withdraw $10 every month, you are going to be paid less earnings on the remaining balance. And if you have nothing you need to buy, where are you going to put that $10? Put it in your piggy bank? How much interest does it earn there? Nothing! So when the government forces you to take money out of your Traditional IRA, you are being forced to give up earnings! If you choose the Roth IRA you can let it grow, and take it out only when you need it.

There is a second great reason to have an investment where you do not have to make mandatory withdrawals. Did you know someone can inherit your IRA? Your IRA is tax-free wealth that you can pass on to you family.

Be sure to designate a beneficiary for your IRA account.

Beneficiary: The person receiving the IRA account when the owner of the account dies.

This means that if something happens to you (if you died), the beneficiary will receive (inherit) your IRA. It is very important to have at least one *designated beneficiary* and one or more *contingent beneficiaries*. The contingent beneficiary is a second person who would receive the IRA if the first person passed away.

In our example, suppose Maria listed her mother as the designated beneficiary and her brother as the contingent beneficiary. If Maria dies, Maria's mother inherits Maria's IRA. If Maria and her mother both die in a car accident, her brother would inherit the IRA.

It is important to see the big difference between Traditional and Roth IRAs when they are inherited.

The big difference should make sense to you from what we have learned so far. The beneficiary of a Traditional IRA has to pay taxes on any money they withdraw but the beneficiary of a Roth IRA can withdraw money tax free! Would you rather inherit a tax-free account or an account you have to pay taxes on? Of course, you want the tax-free Roth IRA!

On the next page, the entire chart is summarized for you.

Roth VS Traditional IRA Comparison Chart for Children

ROTH IRA	TRADITIONAL IRA	Comparison
No age limit to begin contributing.	No age limit to begin contributing.	Same rule for both.
Must have earned income.	Must have earned income.	Same rule for both.
Limited amount may be contributed each year (check with the IRS) and an April 15th deadline of for contributing.	Limited amount may be contributed each year (check with the IRS) and there is an April 15th deadline for contributing.	Same rule for both.
You cannot deduct contributions from taxable income.	You may be able to deduct contributions from taxable income.	**Different rules.**
Your money (contributions and earnings) will grow tax-free.	Your money grows tax deferred. You pay taxes on withdrawals of both earnings and contributions.	**Different rules.**
You can withdraw your *contribution* amount at any time without penalty and without having to pay tax on it.	You pay both a penalty and taxes for withdrawing your contribution amount before age 59½. After age 59½ you pay taxes but no penalty.	**Different rules**
No mandatory distributions. Earnings must be left 5 yrs *and* until age 59½ (unless an exception is met).	Required Mandatory Distributions (RMDs) begin annually before April 1 of the year following the year you turn age 70½.	**Different rules**

So how are you going to open a Roth IRA?

First, you will be sure you have earned income.

Second, as we mentioned, if you are a minor, you must begin with your parents. Ask them to recommend a bank, mutual fund, or brokerage company for your Roth IRA. Your parents will have to sign on the account as your custodian if you are a minor, but the money belongs to you. Be sure to compare investment fees when comparing companies.

Some companies will let you open your Roth IRA as a money market account (very much like a savings account) with little money down. In such cases you can deposit money on a regular basis, as you receive your paychecks. Other companies will require a larger minimum deposit to open a Roth IRA. In this case, you may need to continue depositing your pay into your bank account until you reach the minimum amount needed to open your Roth IRA.

Where are we at in your financial planning? You have earned income and a bank account. You decided you want to put at least part of your earned money into a Roth IRA.

So, how much do you contribute into your Roth IRA? It's up to you. You get to decide how much to contribute into your Roth IRA in accordance with the rules we discussed. You know you cannot contribute more than you have earned and you know there is a limit to how much you can put in each year, but how do you decide how much to contribute?

The toughest decision you will have to make is, "Should you contribute all of your earned income or only part?" We have already explained that your comfort zone and personality will play a role in your financial decisions. You will consider the *time value of money* and you will consider the potential tax-free earnings your account could earn. Lastly, you will consider other items or activities you desire to spend your money on or possibly donating some money to charity.

Pay Yourself First!

Pay Yourself First is one of the many rules you will hear from financially stable individuals. (This idea will help us understand why Maria in the last section put it all in her IRA.)

Pay Yourself First means part of every paycheck goes into savings before making any purchases and before paying any bills. The idea means to set aside some money in savings first and to live on the remainder. Sacrifice today so you can have more tomorrow. This is a financial skill. It takes discipline.

You may think buying that new cell phone is paying yourself first, but it's not. The cell phone is a reward. Paying yourself first means paying in *cash*!

How would you feel if working at *Bob's Burgers*, your boss said, "How about tonight I pay you by giving you a *Bob's Supreme Burger*?"

Would you feel like you were paid? My guess is probably not. I can see kids going home and saying, "Mom, Can you believe he wanted to give me a *Bob's Supreme Burger* instead of cash? I almost quit right there on the spot!"

Well, I want you to treat yourself with the same respect. Pay yourself cash first. Put something in your Roth IRA.

Maria, in the prior example, probably contributed the full amount in her Roth IRA because she did not need to buy anything at the moment. So why not put it all in? It will earn more than in her savings account because the earnings will be growing tax-free!

"But I really want that cell phone."

You tell me, "All my friends have one. I really need one!"

Well, then I want you to budget. And guess what? You have the power to make the final decision because it is your money. But I want you to put at least part of each paycheck toward your Roth IRA. That is the *Pay Yourself First* rule.

Try reading *The Amazing Days of Abby Hayes: Have Wheels, Will Travel* by Anne Mazer if you want a good example of a young lady who spends her money as fast as she receives it and never seems to be able to reach her goal of buying new rollerblades. It is important to always put some money away that you promise not to touch. This is how people build their savings and reach their goals.

It's ok if you don't want to put every penny in. Put some in your savings account to save for the cell phone and contribute the rest to your Roth IRA. A good rule of thumb is to save at least 15 to 20% of your take home paycheck, but if you feel you can save more, by all means do so. The effect of compounding interest will be very powerful for you.

Do you think adults put every penny away into savings? We do not. We have to keep some of our earned money for paying bills, the rent, food, and many more things. It is normal to not save every penny. (But remember, the more you can save, the more you will receive in earnings. It just depends on how much tax-free money you would like to make! The decision is yours.)

Compare saving different fixed amounts each year and how much they grow by age 65 by looking at our next chart.

Looking at the chart, compare the columns. We see a child who started at age 6, contributing $100 a year to a Roth IRA (and contributing that same amount every year after), would have a balance including earnings of $32,258 at retirement. A 16 year old child contributing the same amount will have only $18,703 at retirement.

Now compare across rows to see the difference contribution amounts can make. Who are the millionaires?

The chart makes it very clear that you will have significantly more money by starting early and contributing the same amount on a regular basis.

Roth IRA Contribution Savings Chart

The intersection is the Amount you have at age 65 if you contribute each year earning a 5% return in a 15% tax bracket[23]	$100 each year will grow to:	$500 each year will grow to:	$1,000 each year will grow to:	$2,500 each year will grow to:	$4,000 each year will grow to:
Start at age 6	35,258	176,292	352,584	881,459	1,410,335
Start at age 7	33,479	167,397	334,794	836,985	1,339,176
Start at age 8	31,785	158,926	317,851	794,629	1,271,406
Start at age 9	30,172	150,858	301,716	754,289	1,206,863
Start at age 10	28,635	143,174	286,348	715,871	1,145,393
Start at age 11	27,171	135,856	271,713	679,282	1,086,850
Start at age 12	25,777	128,887	257,774	644,435	1,031,096
Start at age 13	24,450	122,249	244,499	611,247	997,996
Start at age 14	23,186	115,928	231,856	579,640	927,425
Start at age 15	21,982	109,908	219,815	549,538	879,262
Start at age 16	20,835	104,174	208,348	520,870	833,392
Start at age 17	19,743	98,713	197,427	493,567	789,707
Start at age 18	18,703	93,513	187,025	467,563	748,102

---

[23] figures from calculator used at
http://www.dinkytown.net/java/RothIRA.html

Let's also note that the chart figures are definitely on the *low side*. For one thing, the chart assumes a 5% return and it is possible your investment might grow at 6%, 8%, 10% or even higher, if you find a very successful investment.

Also, the chart assumes each child continues to contribute the exact same amount each year which is actually unrealistic. In reality, the amount should increase each year because each year you would likely work more hours and earn more money. If you are following the 20% rule and you earn $100 this year, you would contribute $20 (20% of $100) to your IRA. Next year you might earn $500 and following the rule, you would contribute $100 (20% of $500) to your Roth IRA.

The chart only proves the amount your investment would grow if you consistently invested the *exact same amount* each year at 5% tax-free growth.

So there are many factors playing a role in the final dollar amount one has at retirement. You do have one guarantee. You will not be paying taxes on your Roth IRA investment.

As we stated, you should aim to save at least 15-20% of your earned income. Consistently investing on an annual basis is important. This means contributing the same amount (or greater) every month or year depending on what type of schedule you prefer. (Remember, *Dollar Cost Averaging* will also play a small role with a consistent yearly investment and an even bigger role if you do a monthly investment.)

Keep your contribution amount the same and aim to increase it each year until you have reached the maximum amount you can contribute to your Roth IRA.

This is the idea behind *Pay Yourself First*. Contribute something to your Roth IRA and leave the rest of your paycheck in your savings account. When your saving account reaches your goal amount for that cell phone, reward yourself by making the purchase!

Hands off the Roth! — Withdrawals

Next you tell me, "I don't want anything right now but when I do, can I take my money out of my Roth IRA?"

One flexible thing you learned about a Roth IRA is you can take out what you contributed at any time with no penalty. Of course, the longer you leave it in, the more compound tax-free earnings will be growing. So the best decision is to never withdraw money until you actually retire.

> *Example:* Morgan, age 17, has contributed $300 every year, for 10 years. Her Roth contributions total $3,000 ($300 multiplied by 10 years.) During her senior year of High School, Morgan has a balance of $3,962 in her Roth. $962 of this is earnings ($3,962 balance less $3,000 in contributions).

Morgan's school is sponsoring a summer trip abroad in Europe costing $3,000. Morgan thinks this is a wonderful opportunity not to be passed by. Morgan can withdraw $3,000 from her Roth IRA with no penalty or taxes due because that is the amount of her contributions. But, she cannot withdraw her $962 in earnings without penalties.

Morgan feels good because she has saved, her money has grown tax free, and she has the power (the money) to make the decision to travel. All this is fine but Morgan needs to be reminded again about what *lost opportunity* means.

If Morgan withdraws $3,000, she loses the potential compound earnings and tax-free growth of that money. In other words, it is not costing Morgan $3,000 to go on the trip. It is costing Morgan $3,000 + 48 years of earnings! (Morgan is 17 and in 48 years will be retirement age of 65, so the money will grow 48 more years if Morgan does not withdraw it.)

Imagine how expensive that trip is! How much is $3,000 plus 48 years of compounding tax-free interest? Let's use an online compound interest calculator.

http://www.moneychimp.com/calculator/compound_interest
_calculator.htm

When we enter a one time contribution of $3,000 with $0 additional contributions ever, at a growth of 5% for 48 more years, we find that Morgan's $3,000 could grow to $31,203.81! So, from that perspective, the trip is actually very expensive.

Let's emphasize again that we are discussing withdrawing contributions and not earnings.

Roth Contributions VS Roth Earnings

Contributions may be withdrawn at any time, any age, with no tax or penalty paid.

Earnings can be withdrawn as "Qualified Distributions" or "Early Distributions" where taxes and penalties may apply. (Consult a tax advisor.)

Although this book introduces withdrawal rules, we recommend no withdrawals and a strict policy of keeping your *Hands off the Roth* for maximum tax-free growth.

There is also a 5 year rule, a holding period, applying to Qualified Distributions and several exceptions that may be applicable to help you avoid taxes and/or penalties on early withdrawals. For any withdrawal, consult the IRS or a tax professional to understand any applicable taxes or penalties.

Because contributions can be withdrawn with no penalty, some people use their Roth IRA contributions as a savings plan to save for a first car, an emergency fund, first home (first time home buyer), education, etc. but this was not the government's intention. The intention was to save money for retirement. Before making a withdrawal, remember Morgan's story, and if at all possible, keep your *Hands off the Roth*.

The IRA Gift & the Inherited IRA

There is a phrase floating around, although it is not official, and not found in any IRS documents. It is called *The IRA Gift*. This is an especially bad term because parents and grandparents can be misled into thinking they can give an IRA as a gift. They cannot.

No one can contribute to an IRA, as a gift, to an unmarried child without earned income. If someone claims he received an IRA as a gift, then one of three things has happened.

The first possibility is an IRA account was indeed opened as a gift when the unmarried child had no earned income. In this case, the entire account is illegal and subject to penalty rules for excess contributions.

Excess contributions (you contributed more than you are allowed) are subject to a penalty of a hefty 6% on the amount over-contributed. That's 6% each year! Carefully watch your contribution limit and be sure you have earned income.

The second case of an IRA Gift is legal. An account was indeed opened as a gift for a child but the child had earned income. The child was employed with earned income during the applicable tax year. The parent or grandparent (the person giving the gift) allowed the child to keep his or her hard earned money and the person giving the gift matched the earned income amount (or the IRA contribution limit if that was less than the earned income) in a contribution to an IRA for the child. This is perfectly acceptable.

> *Example:* Michael worked hard mowing lawns all summer and earned $300. Michael's parents told Michael he could keep his $300 and they would put $300 of their own money into an IRA for him.

This kind, generous gesture by his parents leads Michael to call the contribution an IRA Gift. From Michael's perspective it is indeed a gift. He just received an additional $300 bucks! From the IRS perspective, Michael earned $300 and $300 was contributed to his IRA. The IRS does not care exactly where the physical dollars came from as long as Michael earned the same amount.

Now you may ask me, "Can I keep my earned money and ask my parents to contribute an equivalent amount of money, their money, to my IRA?"

Well, yes, you can ask! I am sure you really like that idea. Yes, you can ask your parents if they would like to invest their own money in your future. But most parents and grandparents cannot afford to make your IRA contributions for you. And, remember, in this book, I am trying to teach *you* to be financially independent and *you* to be responsible for your future. Because of this, I would discourage involving your family in your Roth IRA contributions. It is better that you contribute to your IRA on your own with your own hard earned money.

There is one exception. The only time I would recommend asking a parent to help contribute to your Roth IRA is if you bought this book in December and your hard earned money is already spent. Maybe you worked all summer and spent your earned money making purchases and having fun with friends. Your money is long gone. It was spent on enjoyment!

Then, you found this great book and realized you made a big mistake. You are about to lose an opportunity to create a compounding tax-free investment!

Explain to your parents what you have learned, the mistake you unknowingly made, and how you plan to contribute to your Roth IRA next year on your own. Then ask if they might be interested in investing their hard earned money in your future by contributing for you this year.

If they say, "Yes," that is wonderful. But, the fact is they may not have the money either, so maybe they cannot help.

Smart Decisions!

Before parents help fund a Roth IRA for a child, parents should be contributing the maximum amount to their own Roth IRA (assuming they qualify). Parents should take care of their own retirement fund first.

The third way you might refer to your IRA as a gift is if you happen to inherit an IRA. When you inherit an IRA, you (as an unmarried child) will have a few options to choose from. The first option is to cash it all out and re-invest it or spend it. Since this book taught you about tax-free growth, we will assume you would not choose that option.

The second option for children inheriting an IRA is to withdraw distributions from the inherited account over a period of time while the account continues to grow. Consult a tax professional for assistance. You will have two choices:

1. Cash out the entire IRA by December 31 of the fifth year following the death of the original IRA owner.

2. By December 31 of the year after the death of the original IRA owner, start withdrawing a required set amount out each year based on your life expectancy. (The required amount and your life expectancy are determined by the IRS chart in *IRS Publication 590.*)

This book recommends choosing the second choice because this *stretches* the tax-free growth of the inherited IRA account. By only withdrawing a set amount of money each year, you will be taking advantage of continuing compounding tax-free growth on the remaining balance left in the inherited Roth IRA. (Remember the *time value of money!*)

What about Financial Aid for College?

Here's a valid question. When you put money in a Roth IRA, now you have what some may consider an asset, so won't this disqualify you for financial aid for college? You may even hear some people say, "Oh! Don't do that because you might hurt your chances for college financial aid!"

Some colleges do count IRAs as assets and some do not. Federal financial aid forms will be different from Private College financial aid forms. It really just depends on the type of aid you are applying for. It is worth doing some research when you are applying for financial aid. It is not worth passing on the Roth IRA opportunity due to anticipation that a future application form might hold the asset against you.

Would you turn down a job that pays $200,000 just because you might have to pay more taxes? Would you not buy a car because there is a chance you might be in an accident one day? No, certainly not. Well, don't pass on a Roth IRA just because it *might* impact the outcome of a financial aid form.

If for some reason you choose a college that does penalize you for becoming financially independent, for becoming financially responsible, then you will deal with it. You will find another way to pay for college through some other form of aid, scholarships, grants, or student loans. Do not decide to forgo something that is guaranteed in exchange for an "if."

Put money in a Roth IRA and you will have a guarantee. You are guaranteed to be able to withdraw your hard earned dollars with tax-free growth.

This brings us to a second thought, "Are you going to use your Roth IRA to pay for college?" We already said some people do use their Roth IRA as a savings plan, even though the government intends IRAs to be used for retirement.

Remember Morgan who wanted to use $3,000 of her Roth IRA contributions for a summer in Europe? We explained how she would really be paying $31,203.81 due to the lost growth. The same principal applies here.

Besides losing compounding tax-free interest, there is another big problem with using your Roth to pay for college. *You can borrow for college but you can't borrow to retire!*

When you need money for school, there are many places that will help you. When you retire, there are few places that will let you borrow for medical or living expenses. Part of this reason is when you are young, lenders have a good feeling that you will live long enough to pay back the debt. They want their money back! When you are older, at retirement age, lenders may wonder if they will ever receive their money back and thus will not let you easily borrow money.

Please do not use your Roth IRA contributions to pay for college. There are many ways to pay for college. You should research scholarships, grants, and financial aid ideas with your family and guidance counselor. Ask your friends too. Friends may have knowledge from their own parents. There are many more college savings options today than when your parents were growing up. Try all these alternatives before even considering touching any funds in your Roth IRA.

Another alternative source is a student loan. Student loans usually have a very low interest rate (that you will never be able to match if you ever have to borrow money again). If you must borrow, student loans are a good type of debt to have and college is a good reason to borrow money. There are many different types of student loans so look around for the one that suits you best.

So, stick with the rule: *Hands off the Roth!* Try to make no withdrawals until you retire. You will most likely need your money then.

What about 529 Plans, Bonds, or Other Investments?

You will at some time in your life hear opinions from others telling you where you should invest your money. Friends and family might recommend you invest in something called a 529 Plan, you might hear about a 401K plan at work, or you might hear about government savings bonds and state bonds.

There are many, many types of investments and even more people who will are willing to share their view on which is best. If you would like to learn more about investing, you should read some of the resources at the end of this book. Many of the books may be found at your local library.

This book recommends the Roth IRA as a first investment because we are focused on unmarried children with no dependents and a small annual salary. The questions will come, "Why did you choose the Roth IRA for your money? Why didn't you invest in (fill in a type of investment here)?"

Listen carefully to what others say because once you have contributed the maximum amount to your Roth IRA, the next step is to look further for the best investment for the rest of your money. When looking at additional investments to the Roth IRA, there are several questions to consider:

1. *Does the investment earn tax-free interest?* In a Roth IRA both your contributions and earnings grow tax free.

2. *Can you remove your contribution amounts at any time without paying a penalty or taxes?* A Roth IRA allows you to withdraw contributions for any reason.

3. *How does the investment pass to your heirs?* A Roth IRA can pass as a tax-free investment on to your designated beneficiary who can then benefit from future compounding tax-free earnings.

4. *Are you required to withdraw money at any time?* You are never forced to take money out of your Roth IRA.

5. *Can you contribute your entire life?* Age is not a factor in a Roth. As long as you have earned income and are not limited by your modified adjusted gross income (under $114,000 for 2007), you may contribute.

6. *If you are looking at an investment with an educational benefit, what happens if you do not use the money for education?* A 529 Plan or government bonds are some investments where withdrawals are tax free if used for college or higher education. Your Roth IRA has exceptions for education too. However, if you do not use your Roth IRA for education, (if you use a grant, scholarship, financial aid, or student loan) there are still no taxes due! This is not true of some alternative investments. For the most flexibility, if you have the earned income to do so, fund your Roth IRA to the maximum amount allowed. Then, if you have funds remaining, consider opening a 529 Plan for college.

Note: A 529 Plan is an excellent way for your parents and extended family members to save *their money* to help pay for your higher education. (They should fully fund their own IRA first and then open a 529 Plan for you.)

7. *Is the investment a company matching 401K plan?* Some companies offer a 401K matching retirement plan. Matching means the company will contribute the same amount of money you do (up to a certain amount). If you contribute $100, the company will match (give you) $100, so your balance will be $200. Participating is an easy way to double your money and a very good step to take when you work for a company that offers a 401K plan.

Tax Talk — All about Forms

To avoid this book becoming extremely long, we do not repeat information applicable to more than one section but instead, tax instructions will build on instructions from prior tax sections. Therefore, *it is best to read the tax sections in order.*

We have gone over some of the differences between a Roth and a Traditional IRA. Now, we will discuss more about how to do taxes applicable to each of the particular job types we have described earlier.

"But I'm not doing taxes! I don't want to do taxes!"

You may say, "I'm too young!" Well, guess what? There is no age requirement for filing a tax return. Everyone must pay taxes depending on the amount of annual income earned.

Almost everyone does not want to do taxes! The few exceptions are those that work in accounting fields such as your tax professionals and auditors. Perhaps you are an exception with a love of math and will soon realize preparing taxes could be an enjoyable future part time job.

We all file taxes and this is an important step for you to take toward becoming financially independent as well as obeying the law. Since you are young and have a much smaller amount of earned income than most adults, I am going to teach you to do your taxes yourself. Taxes are not very complex when your income is low so you should be able to complete them yourself.

Depending on your income, you may not be required to file a tax return. I am not going to teach you the rules where you do not have to file. Why? Because I think you should always file. It establishes good financial records and you can be sure you are not overlooking a refund that may be due to you.

Did you know there are cases where you do not have to file taxes and the IRS owes you a refund? If you do not file, you will never receive your refund. The IRS isn't going to chase you down to give you your money.

Why doesn't the IRS tell you that you have a refund? Because, they don't know you are due a refund. How come they don't know? They don't know because you didn't file your taxes. If you don't report your unique circumstances, the IRS can't know that you are due money back.

So when you say, "I don't want to do taxes," I will say, "Yes, you do. You just do not know it yet."

Remember our goal in this book is to teach you what to do once you have a job, to encourage you to invest in your own Individual Retirement Account, a Roth IRA.

The easiest way to contribute to a Roth IRA is to begin with good financial records of your employment. Filing taxes creates good financial records of your work history and documents your earned income.

So, the first two reasons to file your taxes are: to have good financial records and to be sure you receive a refund if one is due to you.

A third reason to file is you will gain more experience in dealing with financial issues, which will educate you to make even better financial decisions for the future. This education will be very valuable as your taxes become more complex. You will become so familiar with the forms that adding information such as owning a house or having a second job will not seem as challenging as it would be for others.

A fourth reason to file your taxes is it will be a double check for you that you have not over contributed to your Roth IRA. You will know exactly what figure to use to determine the maximum amount you can contribute for the year.

What is the figure you use for earned income?

We are going to go over taxes for each type of job so you can answer this question and know which figure to use.

How to Complete a Form W-4

The first type of tax document you will encounter is the Form W-4, *Employee's Withholding Allowance Certificate*. When you are hired, your employer will give you a Form W-4 to complete. Below is a picture of the middle and bottom of the form which is enough for us to see what needs to be completed. Images in this book are for quick reference only. Please use a real form from **www.irs.gov** with large print.

Personal Allowances Worksheet (Keep for your records.)

A Enter "1" for **yourself** if no one else can claim you as a dependent . . . . **A** ____

B Enter "1" if:
- You are single and have only one job; or
- You are married, have only one job, and your spouse does not work; or
- Your wages from a second job or your spouse's wages (or the total of both) are $1,000 or less.

. . **B** ____

C Enter "1" for your **spouse**. But, you may choose to enter "-0-" if you are married and have either a working spouse or more than one job. (Entering "-0-" may help you avoid having too little tax withheld.) . . . . **C** ____

D Enter number of **dependents** (other than your spouse or yourself) you will claim on your tax return . . . . . . **D** ____

E Enter "1" if you will file as **head of household** on your tax return (see conditions under **Head of household** above) . **E** ____

F Enter "1" if you have at least $1,500 of **child or dependent care expenses** for which you plan to claim a credit . . **F** ____
(**Note. Do not** include child support payments. See Pub. 503, Child and Dependent Care Expenses, for details.)

G **Child Tax Credit** (including additional child tax credit). See Pub 972, Child Tax Credit, for more information.
- If your total income will be less than $57,000 ($85,000 if married), enter "2" for each eligible child.
- If your total income will be between $57,000 and $84,000 ($85,000 and $119,000 if married), enter "1" for each eligible child plus "1" **additional** if you have 4 or more eligible children. . . . . **G** ____

H Add lines A through G and enter total here. (**Note.** This may be different from the number of exemptions you claim on your tax return.) ▶ **H** ____

For accuracy, complete all worksheets that apply.
- If you plan to **itemize or claim adjustments to income** and want to reduce your withholding, see the **Deductions and Adjustments Worksheet** on page 2.
- If you have **more than one job** or are **married and you and your spouse both work** and the combined earnings from all jobs exceed $40,000 ($25,000 if married) see the **Two-Earners/Multiple Jobs Worksheet** on page 2 to avoid having too little tax withheld.
- If **neither** of the above situations applies, **stop here** and enter the number from line H on line 5 of Form W-4 below.

- - - - - - - - - - - - - - **Cut here and give Form W-4 to your employer. Keep the top part for your records.** - - - - - - - - - - - - - -

Form **W-4**	**Employee's Withholding Allowance Certificate**	OMB No. 1545-0074
Department of the Treasury Internal Revenue Service	▶ Whether you are entitled to claim a certain number of allowances or exemption from withholding is subject to review by the IRS. Your employer may be required to send a copy of this form to the IRS.	**2007**

1 Type or print your first name and middle initial.	Last name	2 Your social security number

Home address (number and street or rural route)	3 ☐ Single ☐ Married ☐ Married, but withhold at higher Single rate. Note. If married, but legally separated, or spouse is a nonresident alien, check the "Single" box.
City or town, state, and ZIP code	4 **If your last name differs from that shown on your social security card, check here. You must call 1-800-772-1213 for a replacement card.** ▶ ☐

5 Total number of allowances you are claiming (from line **H** above **or** from the applicable worksheet on page 2) **5** ____

6 Additional amount, if any, you want withheld from each paycheck . . . . **6** $ ____

7 I claim exemption from withholding for 2007, and I certify that I meet **both** of the following conditions for exemption.
- Last year I had a right to a refund of **all** federal income tax withheld because I had **no** tax liability **and**
- This year I expect a refund of **all** federal income tax withheld because I expect to have **no** tax liability.
If you meet both conditions, write "Exempt" here . . . . ▶ **7**

Under penalties of perjury, I declare that I have examined this certificate and to the best of my knowledge and belief, it is true, correct, and complete.

Employee's signature
(Form is not valid unless you sign it.) ▶ _____ Date ▶ _____

8 Employer's name and address (Employer: Complete lines 8 and 10 only if sending to the IRS.)	9 Office code (optional)	10 Employer identification number (EIN)

| For Privacy Act and Paperwork Reduction Act Notice, see page 2. | Cat. No. 10220Q | Form **W-4** (2007) |

You will complete the very bottom, *Employee's Withholding Allowance Certificate*, cut it off from the page, and give it to your employer. Again, because you are young, things become fairly simple which makes completing the form easier.

By completing this form, you tell your employer how much tax to withhold from your paycheck. If you complete the form incorrectly and too little tax is withheld, you will end up owing taxes when you file your tax return. If you complete the form incorrectly and too much tax is withheld, then you will have a nice refund when you file your return by the due date of April 15th. The only bad thing about a nice big refund is you receive it without interest. In other words, if you had not withheld too much but instead received that money during the year, you could have earned interest on it in either your bank savings account or Roth IRA!

To complete the form, start with the bottom certificate:

- Number 1: Enter name, address, city, state and zip code.
- Number 2: Enter your Social Security number. Be sure to write this correctly. Try to memorize your number.
- Number 3: You will check single unless for some reason you were able to marry at a young age. (If you are married, many rules change. This book assumes you are not married. You can still use the book as a general reference, a starting point, but will need to consult with a tax advisor on how the rules differ if you are married.)
- Number 4: Leave blank since your name should match your Social Security card.
- Number 5: We need to use the worksheet to figure out what to put in entry number 5. The worksheet is on the top of the Form W-4 right above the certificate. We use the worksheet to figure out personal allowances. This is the number that tells the employer how much tax to withhold. Let's look line by line at the worksheet.
  - Line A: "Enter "1" for yourself if no one else can claim you as a dependent." Your parents should be claiming you as a dependent. You are their dependent. Leave Line A blank.

o Line B: Enter 1 if you are single and have only one job or if you have two jobs and the second job pays you less than $1,000 for the year. Most young adults will have an entry of 1 on Line B.

o Lines C through G: Leave blank because they are not applicable to you, an unmarried child with no dependents of your own.

o Line H. Add up the lines. Most young adults will have an entry of 1 on Line H.

Pause a minute and look at that form. There was a lot of reading and a lot of issues, but since you are young, they do not apply to you. This makes the form relatively easy to fill out. Do not become overwhelmed by all the text and words. Rest assured a lot of it will not even apply to you!

Now, that you have figured out your personal allowance, take the number from H (which is probably 1) and enter it on Number 5 on the actual W-4 Form.

- Number 6: If you want more money withheld you would put an amount here. In most cases, leave this line blank.

- Number 7: "I claim exemption from withholding and I certify that I meet both of the following conditions for exemption." This means you *must* meet both of the conditions to claim *Exempt*. *Exempt* means your employer will *not* withhold any federal tax from your pay. Write "*Exempt*" on Number 7 if you meet the two conditions:

    1. The first condition is that you had no tax liability last year. Well, if this is your first job, then you definitely had no tax liability last year so you meet the first condition. If this is your second year or more of working, then you will know from your past tax returns if you owed taxes last year.

2. The second condition is that you expect not to owe taxes this year. Your employer will know roughly what your salary will be for the year and can help you answer this question. (If you will earn less than the single standard deduction for the year, then you can expect not to owe taxes.)

Did you know?

In the case where you will work for your parents in their self-employed business (sole proprietorship or spouse partnership) or as a household employee, if you are not working significant hours and not earning annual pay over the amount of the single standard deduction amount, you should write "Exempt" on this line. (This makes paperwork a lot easier for your parents because they will not have to withhold federal taxes.)

- Finally: Add your signature and date, cut the form from the instructions, hand it to your employer and you are finished!

Let's review what you did. You have your job and you completed your Form W-4 by entering personal information, computing your personal allowances for Line 5 and signing the form. Next, give it to your employer.

Are you getting comfortable? You will realize as we go through this book that difficult is not an accurate word to describe working, saving, and filing taxes. A better word is uncomfortable. Many adults are also uncomfortable with the unknown or with things they do not do everyday. You should use this book, along with the IRA publications to become not only comfortable, but also confident that you are working, saving, and filing taxes in accordance with the law.

The Form W-2, Wage and Tax Statement

22222	Void ☐	a Employee's social security number	For Official Use Only ▶ OMB No. 1545-0008		
b Employer identification number (EIN)			1 Wages, tips, other compensation	2 Federal income tax withheld	
c Employer's name, address, and ZIP code			3 Social security wages	4 Social security tax withheld	
			5 Medicare wages and tips	6 Medicare tax withheld	
			7 Social security tips	8 Allocated tips	
d Control number			9 Advance EIC payment	10 Dependent care benefits	
e Employee's first name and initial	Last name	Suff.	11 Nonqualified plans	12a See instructions for box 12
			13 Statutory employee ☐ Retirement plan ☐ Third-party sick pay ☐	12b
			14 Other	12c
				12d
f Employee's address and ZIP code				
15 State Employer's state ID number	16 State wages, tips, etc.	17 State income tax	18 Local wages, tips, etc.	19 Local income tax	20 Locality name

Form **W-2** Wage and Tax Statement

2007

Department of the Treasury—Internal Revenue Service

Copy A For Social Security Administration — Send this entire page with Form W-3 to the Social Security Administration; photocopies are **not** acceptable.

For Privacy Act and Paperwork Reduction Act Notice, see back of Copy D.

Cat. No. 10134D

Do Not Cut, Fold, or Staple Forms on This Page — Do Not Cut, Fold, or Staple Forms on This Page

Form W-2 99

If you are not self-employed, you will be given a *Form W-2, Wage and Tax Statement* from your employer. This is a form your employer provides at the end of the year summarizing all the money you have received for all the hard work you have done. Every form has the same entry boxes. Sometimes the boxes are printed in different locations on the form, so your Form W-2 may not look exactly like our sample on the previous page but it will have the same boxes: A through E and 1 though 20.

For most employed children:

- Boxes A through E will contain information about your employer and you (the employee) such as name, address, and Social Security number.
- Boxes 1 through 20 all have to do with what your employer will pay you.
- Box 1 will have your wages paid and Box 2 has how much federal tax your employer withheld.
- Box 3 will contain the amount of your wages taxed for Social Security.
- Box 4 has the amount your employer withheld for Social Security.
- Box 5 and 6 follow in a similar manner, the first being wages subjected to Medicare tax and then, the actual Medicare tax amount withheld.
- Boxes 11 through 14 are usually for employer related plans and will usually be blank on a child's Form W-2.
- You might also have entries in Boxes 15 through 20 (if your employer withholds state and local taxes).

At this point, you should just understand that a Form W-2 is a summary of your wages for the entire year. You should also be aware that you will receive one from your employer. Don't worry too much about the entries right now. We will discuss that later when we go through some tax examples.

Tax Overview — Use Form 1040

The first step to doing taxes is to stop by your library. Each year libraries hand out the current Form 1040, Federal Tax Return instruction booklets. You will use this to file your tax return. They hand these out for you to keep. You do not borrow them like other library books. You can keep and write on the instruction booklet and form.

Take a quick peek at the Form 1040 on the next two pages. You don't have to read every line but you can see what the tax form looks like.

Now, you will hear some people tell you, "You don't need to use that big long form. There is a form called 1040 EZ that you can use or even the Form 1040A." That EZ on the end of the title of the Form 1040 EZ, which sounds like *easy* is just that. It is a simpler form that people use when their taxes are not complex. The 1040A is a second type of simpler form.

Well, here is the problem, if I teach you on the simple form, then when you have a more complex issue you will need to learn the Form 1040 anyway, so why not learn it from the start? This way I only have to teach you one method and teach you once. The complex Form 1040 has lines for the same entries that the Form 1040EZ and Form 1040A have. The Form 1040 will cover any financial situation in your entire life, so let's learn to use it.

And guess what? If you are doing your own taxes, all the forms are free and cost you the same amount to mail them in to the IRS. So, the cost, if you are preparing your own taxes, is the same.

You may say, "I don't want to look at all those lines, all that tiny print. This is too difficult!"

Is it difficult or uncomfortable? This book and your parents will help you complete your information.

The front of the 2007 Form 1040 looks like this:

Form **1040**

Department of the Treasury—Internal Revenue Service

U.S. Individual Income Tax Return **2007**

IRS Use Only—Do not write or staple in this space.

For the year Jan. 1–Dec. 31, 2007, or other tax year beginning , 2007, ending , 20

OMB No. 1545-0074

Label
(See instructions on page 12.)
Use the IRS label. Otherwise, please print or type.

L A B E L

H E R E

Your first name and initial | Last name | Your social security number

If a joint return, spouse's first name and initial | Last name | Spouse's social security number

Home address (number and street). If you have a P.O. box, see page 12. | Apt. no. | ▲ You **must** enter your SSN(s) above. ▲

City, town or post office, state, and ZIP code. If you have a foreign address, see page 12. | Checking a box below will not change your tax or refund.

Presidential Election Campaign ▶ Check here if you, or your spouse if filing jointly, want $3 to go to this fund (see page 12) ▶ ☐ You ☐ Spouse

Filing Status
Check only one box.

1 ☐ Single
2 ☐ Married filing jointly (even if only one had income)
3 ☐ Married filing separately. Enter spouse's SSN above and full name here. ▶
4 ☐ Head of household (with qualifying person). (See page 13.) If the qualifying person is a child but not your dependent, enter this child's name here. ▶
5 ☐ Qualifying widow(er) with dependent child (see page 14)

Exemptions

6a ☐ **Yourself.** If someone can claim you as a dependent, **do not** check box 6a
b ☐ **Spouse**
c Dependents:

(1) First name Last name	(2) Dependent's social security number	(3) Dependent's relationship to you	(4) ✔ if qualifying child for child tax credit (see page 15)
			☐
			☐
			☐
			☐

If more than four dependents, see page 15.

d Total number of exemptions claimed

Boxes checked on 6a and 6b
No. of children on 6c who:
• lived with you
• did not live with you due to divorce or separation (see page 18)
Dependents on 6c not entered above
Add numbers on lines above ▶

Income

Attach Form(s) W-2 here. Also attach Forms W-2G and 1099-R if tax was withheld.

If you did not get a W-2, see page 19.

Enclose, but do not attach, any payment. Also, please use Form 1040-V.

7 Wages, salaries, tips, etc. Attach Form(s) W-2 | 7
8a Taxable interest. Attach Schedule B if required | 8a
b Tax-exempt interest. **Do not** include on line 8a | 8b
9a Ordinary dividends. Attach Schedule B if required | 9a
b Qualified dividends (see page 19) | 9b
10 Taxable refunds, credits, or offsets of state and local income taxes (see page 20) | 10
11 Alimony received | 11
12 Business income or (loss). Attach Schedule C or C-EZ | 12
13 Capital gain or (loss). Attach Schedule D if required. If not required, check here ▶ ☐ | 13
14 Other gains or (losses). Attach Form 4797 | 14
15a IRA distributions | 15a | b Taxable amount (see page 21) | 15b
16a Pensions and annuities | 16a | b Taxable amount (see page 22) | 16b
17 Rental real estate, royalties, partnerships, S corporations, trusts, etc. Attach Schedule E | 17
18 Farm income or (loss). Attach Schedule F | 18
19 Unemployment compensation | 19
20a Social security benefits | 20a | b Taxable amount (see page 24) | 20b
21 Other income. List type and amount (see page 24) | 21
22 Add the amounts in the far right column for lines 7 through 21. This is your **total income** ▶ | 22

Adjusted Gross Income

23 Educator expenses (see page 26) | 23
24 Certain business expenses of reservists, performing artists, and fee-basis government officials. Attach Form 2106 or 2106-EZ | 24
25 Health savings account deduction. Attach Form 8889 | 25
26 Moving expenses. Attach Form 3903 | 26
27 One-half of self-employment tax. Attach Schedule SE | 27
28 Self-employed SEP, SIMPLE, and qualified plans | 28
29 Self-employed health insurance deduction (see page 26) | 29
30 Penalty on early withdrawal of savings | 30
31a Alimony paid b Recipient's SSN ▶ | 31a
32 IRA deduction (see page 27) | 32
33 Student loan interest deduction (see page 30) | 33
34 Tuition and fees deduction. Attach Form 8917 | 34
35 Domestic production activities deduction. Attach Form 8903 | 35
36 Add lines 23 through 31a and 32 through 35 ▶ | 36
37 Subtract line 36 from line 22. This is your **adjusted gross income** ▶ | 37

For Disclosure, Privacy Act, and Paperwork Reduction Act Notice, see page 83.

Cat. No. 11320B

Form **1040** (2007)

The back of the 2007 Form 1040 looks like this:

Tax and Credits	38	Amount from line 37 (adjusted gross income)	38
	39a	Check { ☐ **You** were born before January 2, 1943, ☐ Blind. } Total boxes if: { ☐ **Spouse** was born before January 2, 1943, ☐ Blind. } checked ▶ 39a	
Standard Deduction for—	b	If your spouse itemizes on a separate return or you were a dual-status alien, see page 31 and check here ▶39b ☐	
	40	**Itemized deductions** (from Schedule A) **or** your **standard deduction** (see left margin) . .	40
	41	Subtract line 40 from line 38	41
• People who checked any box on line 39a or 39b or who can be claimed as a dependent, see page 31.	42	If line 38 is $117,300 or less, multiply $3,400 by the total number of exemptions claimed on line 6d. If line 38 is over $117,300, see the worksheet on page 33	42
	43	**Taxable income.** Subtract line 42 from line 41. If line 42 is more than line 41, enter -0- .	43
	44	**Tax** (see page 33). Check if any tax is from: **a** ☐ Form(s) 8814 **b** ☐ Form 4972 **c** ☐ Form(s) 8889	44
• All others:	45	**Alternative minimum tax** (see page 36). Attach Form 6251	45
Single or Married filing separately, $5,350	46	Add lines 44 and 45 . . . . ▶	46
	47	Credit for child and dependent care expenses. Attach Form 2441	47	
	48	Credit for the elderly or the disabled. Attach Schedule R .	48	
Married filing jointly or Qualifying widow(er), $10,700	49	Education credits. Attach Form 8863	49	
	50	Residential energy credits. Attach Form 5695	50	
	51	Foreign tax credit. Attach Form 1116 if required . . .	51	
Head of household, $7,850	52	Child tax credit (see page 39). Attach Form 8901 if required	52	
	53	Retirement savings contributions credit. Attach Form 8880 .	53	
	54	Credits from: **a** ☐ Form 8396 **b** ☐ Form 8859 **c** ☐ Form 8839	54	
	55	Other credits: **a** ☐ Form 3800 **b** ☐ Form 8801 **c** ☐ Form_____	55	
	56	Add lines 47 through 55. These are your **total credits**	56
	57	Subtract line 56 from line 46. If line 56 is more than line 46, enter -0- . . . . ▶	57
Other Taxes	58	Self-employment tax. Attach Schedule SE	58
	59	Unreported social security and Medicare tax from: **a** ☐ Form 4137 **b** ☐ Form 8919 .	59
	60	Additional tax on IRAs, other qualified retirement plans, etc. Attach Form 5329 if required . .	60
	61	Advance earned income credit payments from Form(s) W-2, box 9	61
	62	Household employment taxes. Attach Schedule H	62
	63	Add lines 57 through 62. This is your **total tax** . . . . ▶	63
Payments	64	Federal income tax withheld from Forms W-2 and 1099 . .	64	
	65	2007 estimated tax payments and amount applied from 2006 return	65	
If you have a qualifying child, attach Schedule EIC.	66a	**Earned income credit (EIC)**	66a	
	b	Nontaxable combat pay election ▶ 66b		
	67	Excess social security and tier 1 RRTA withheld (see page 59)	67	
	68	Additional child tax credit. Attach Form 8812	68	
	69	Amount paid with request for extension to file (see page 59)	69	
	70	Payments from: **a** ☐ Form 2439 **b** ☐ Form 4136 **c** ☐ Form 8885 .	70	
	71	Refundable credit for prior year minimum tax from Form 8801, line 27	71	
	72	Add lines 64, 65, 66a, and 67 through 71. These are your **total payments** . . . . ▶	72
Refund	73	If line 72 is more than line 63, subtract line 63 from line 72. This is the amount you **overpaid**	73
Direct deposit? See page 59 and fill in 74b, 74c, and 74d, or Form 8888.	74a	Amount of line 73 you want **refunded to you.** If Form 8888 is attached, check here ▶ ☐	74a
	▶ b	Routing number [ ] ▶ c Type: ☐ Checking ☐ Savings	
	▶ d	Account number [ ]	
	75	Amount of line 73 you want **applied to your 2008 estimated tax** ▶	75	
Amount You Owe	76	**Amount you owe.** Subtract line 72 from line 63. For details on how to pay, see page 60 ▶	76
	77	Estimated tax penalty (see page 61)	77	
Third Party Designee	Do you want to allow another person to discuss this return with the IRS (see page 61)? ☐ **Yes.** Complete the following. ☐ **No**		
	Designee's name ▶	Phone no. ▶ ( )	Personal identification number (PIN) ▶ [ ]
Sign Here Joint return? See page 13. Keep a copy for your records.	Under penalties of perjury, I declare that I have examined this return and accompanying schedules and statements, and to the best of my knowledge and belief, they are true, correct, and complete. Declaration of preparer (other than taxpayer) is based on all information of which preparer has any knowledge.		
	Your signature	Date	Your occupation	Daytime phone number ( )
	Spouse's signature. If a joint return, **both** must sign.	Date	Spouse's occupation	
Paid Preparer's Use Only	Preparer's signature ▶	Date	Check if self-employed ☐	Preparer's SSN or PTIN
	Firm's name (or yours if self-employed), address, and ZIP code ▶		EIN	
			Phone no. ( )	

Form **1040** (2007)

Remember, the images in this book are just for quick reference. I expect you to use a real form which is 8.5 by 11 inches so the print will be much easier to read.

Let me emphasize, I want you to have the actual form. Do not do your taxes with a computer program, at least not when you first start.

First of all, that will cost you money, assuming you buy the program. But even if you can qualify for one of the free computer programs, I want you to understand the form itself so you understand where everything goes. This way you will know if the computer makes a mistake!

Well, okay, computers don't really make a mistake unless you enter something incorrectly, but that is my point. If you answer a computer question incorrectly because you did not understand what the computer was asking, you can really make a big mess of your taxes. So, learn by using the form itself. Someday, when you do decide to use computer software, your only challenge will be, "How do I tell the computer to put this entry on line (enter a form line number here)?"

By using the actual form, and the more complex form, you will become familiar with it, gain experience using it, and be prepared for a time in your life when finances become more complex. As your finances become more complex with investments and home ownership, you *must* use the form 1040. So why not learn it now?

You can use the Form 1040 no matter what job you have and no matter what your income level is. The Form 1040 will *always* work. You cannot say that about other forms. Best of all, by using the Form 1040, you will become comfortable with it and using it will no longer feel difficult!

In the next sections we will use the Form 1040 to complete tax returns for different types of jobs.

Taxes for Job Type 1: Employer – Employee Relationship

So, you received your Form W-2 from your employer, which means, it is time to do your taxes. The best way to learn is going to be by using an example of someone working in an Employer-Employee relationship type of job.

> **Example:** You worked at Pete's Pizza. You did not spend any of your money but deposited every paycheck in your savings account. You earned $8.32 in interest in your savings account. You did not claim *Exempt* on your Form W-4. In January, your boss gives you a Form W-2 that has these 2007 entries:

1 Wages, tips, other compensation	2 Federal income tax withheld
1,370.36	137.04
3 Social security wages	4 Social security tax withheld
1,370.36	84.96
5 Medicare wages and tips	6 Medicare tax withheld
1,370.36	19.87

Let's do your taxes. You have your Form 1040 instruction book that you picked up at your local library, which has the Form 1040 inside. Take out the form and begin at the top. You can and should read the instruction booklet along with this book. You can also seek advice from a tax expert or your parents if something is confusing. Use pencil for your taxes until you are sure there are no mistakes. This is why instructions usually come with two sets of forms, one to work in pencil and the second to finalize in ink.

Label Section: Enter your full name, address and Social Security number on the form. If you do not know your Social Security number, ask your parents and try to memorize your number as you will need it throughout your life.

The next question asks if you want $3 to go to the Presidential Election Campaign fund. The answer will not change your tax due or refund amount. Checking the box means "yes," the government will give $3 to help candidates with their election campaigns. Leaving it blank means no money will be given. If you want funds given, check the box.

Filing Status: This book is written for unmarried employed children with no dependents. (You can follow along if you are married or have dependents, but then consult a tax advisor to ask about differences. It is just a little different if you are married or have dependents. It usually means receiving a larger refund.) Again, since we are assuming you are not married, put an "X" in the Single box on Line 1.

Exemptions: This next section is where the IRS wants to know if you are supporting someone else (like if you have a child) or if someone is supporting you (like your parents).

(Again, we are assuming you are an employed unmarried child responsible only for yourself, with no children. If you have a child, please consult a tax advisor as there are many tax credits (these are good) that might apply to you.)

If you have no children and your parents support you, you will leave this section blank because your parents will be claiming you as a dependent. You cannot claim yourself if your parents can claim you as a dependent. Enter your total exemptions on Line 6d, in the box to the far right. Enter 0 in Box 6d.

Income: The next section on the form is everything related to Income. This section includes Lines 7 through 22. Even before reading any of the tiny print, let's think about what money you received this year.

Well, we know you received income from your employer, and you also received some interest on you savings account. Remember interest from a savings account is taxable.

You might remember, you also have earnings from your Roth IRA but remember these earnings are tax-free. You do not have to report them at all. (The benefits of your Roth IRA should become even clearer now that you see the tax form.)

All you have to do is figure out on what line to report your income from your employer (wages) and on what line to report your interest income.

Looking at the form, we see there is Line 7 called *Wages, salaries, tips, etc. Attach Forms W-2*. This is where you will report the income from your Employer — Employee job.

For Line 7, we need the amount of your wages. The amount comes from Box 1 of your Form W-2 that you received from your employer. (Remember, in the example, we gave you a picture of this part of your Form W-2.) Copy the amount in Box 1 of the Form W-2 onto Line 7 of your Form 1040. Write $1,370 on Line 7. Tax returns round to the nearest dollar and .36 is less than .50 so we round down. That's it for wages.

Now we need to report your interest. In the Income section of the Form 1040, we see Line 8a, called *Taxable Interest*. This is where your interest goes.

Banks must send you a Form 1099-INT if you earn more than $10 interest. If you received an interest statement from your bank, you can copy the amount of interest from this statement onto the Form 1040, Line 8a.

If you have no Form 1099-INT, you still have to tell the IRS about your savings account interest. If you did not receive any document from your bank, you can call your bank and ask how much interest you earned this year.

We told you in the example that you earned $8.32 in interest, so write $8 on Line 8a. (You round down again since .32 is less than 50.)

That's all for reporting your income. Completing those two lines!

Do you need to read all the other fine print lines in the income section? Well, you can and probably should. It might even be fun to look now since you know none of it applies to you. You can read to have knowledge of things to come as you grow older and have more complicated finances.

We made the income section simpler by thinking before we read. We thought, "What do I need to tell the IRS?" This is easier than reading and wondering, "Do I have that? Does that apply to me?" or "What is that?"

Start with yourself. You know what money you have because, let's face it, you don't have that much yet, and this fact makes taxes fairly simple.

Skim the rest of the income lines to just be aware of things you may become involved with as you grow older, have a different type of job, or win the lottery! Lottery winnings or prizes go on Line 21, *Other Income*. You can also read more in the Form 1040 instructions.

Next, go to the last line of the income section, Line 22, and add all lines above it to arrive at your total income for the year. Enter $1,378 on Line 22.

Adjusted Gross Income: Under certain circumstances the government will let you reduce your taxable income and this whole section applies to that. A good example we learned about was the Traditional IRA. If you had chosen to contribute to a Traditional IRA, you would enter the amount in this section, on Line 32. It would be subtracted from your total income, thus reducing your taxable income.

But, you chose a Roth IRA so you have no deductions. Complete the last two lines in this section. Line 36 is balnk, because you are totaling Lines 23 through 36 which are blank, and after doing the math, Line 37 is $1,378 which is called your Adjusted Gross Income (AGI). (In your case, your income was not adjusted because we had nothing to subtract out, no adjustments to make.)

Wow! You finished the first page! Congratulations! Your form should look like this:

Form **1040**	Department of the Treasury—Internal Revenue Service	U.S. Individual Income Tax Return	**2007**		IRS Use Only—Do not write or staple in this space.	

For the year Jan. 1–Dec. 31, 2007, or other tax year beginning ____ , 2007, ending ____ , 20 ____   OMB No. 1545-0074

Label (See instructions on page 12.) Use the IRS label. Otherwise, please print or type.

Your first name and initial: **YOUR FIRST NAME**   Last name: **YOUR LAST NAME**   Your social security number: **YOUR # HERE**

If a joint return, spouse's first name and initial ____ Last name ____   Spouse's social security number

Home address (number and street). If you have a P.O. box, see page 12. **YOUR STREET ADDRESS**   Apt. no. ____

▲ You **must** enter your SSN(s) above. ▲

City, town or post office, state, and ZIP code. If you have a foreign address, see page 12. **YOUR CITY, YOUR STATE   YOUR ZIP CODE**

Checking a box below will not change your tax or refund.

Presidential Election Campaign ▶ Check here if you, or your spouse if filing jointly, want $3 to go to this fund (see page 12) ▶   [X] You   [ ] Spouse

Filing Status
Check only one box.

1. [X] Single
2. [ ] Married filing jointly (even if only one had income)
3. [ ] Married filing separately. Enter spouse's SSN above and full name here. ▶
4. [ ] Head of household (with qualifying person). (See page 13.) If the qualifying person is a child but not your dependent, enter this child's name here. ▶
5. [ ] Qualifying widow(er) with dependent child (see page 14)

Exemptions

6a [ ] **Yourself.** If someone can claim you as a dependent, **do not** check box 6a
b [ ] **Spouse**

Boxes checked on 6a and 6b ____

c Dependents:

(1) First name Last name	(2) Dependent's social security number	(3) Dependent's relationship to you	(4) ✓ if qualifying child for child tax credit (see page 15)
			[ ]
			[ ]
			[ ]
			[ ]

No. of children on 6c who:
• lived with you ____
• did not live with you due to divorce or separation (see page 16) ____

Dependents on 6c not entered above ____

If more than four dependents, see page 15.

d Total number of exemptions claimed

Add numbers on lines above ▶ **0**

Income

Attach Form(s) W-2 here. Also attach Forms W-2G and 1099-R if tax was withheld.

If you did not get a W-2, see page 19.

Enclose, but do not attach, any payment. Also, please use Form 1040-V.

7 Wages, salaries, tips, etc. Attach Form(s) W-2 7   **1,370**
8a Taxable interest. Attach Schedule B if required 8a   **8**
b Tax-exempt interest. Do not include on line 8a 8b
9a Ordinary dividends. Attach Schedule B if required 9a
b Qualified dividends (see page 19) 9b
10 Taxable refunds, credits, or offsets of state and local income taxes (see page 20) . 10
11 Alimony received 11
12 Business income or (loss). Attach Schedule C or C-EZ 12
13 Capital gain or (loss). Attach Schedule D if required. If not required, check here ▶ [ ] 13
14 Other gains or (losses). Attach Form 4797 14
15a IRA distributions .... 15a ____ b Taxable amount (see page 21) 15b
16a Pensions and annuities 16a ____ b Taxable amount (see page 22) 16b
17 Rental real estate, royalties, partnerships, S corporations, trusts, etc. Attach Schedule E 17
18 Farm income or (loss). Attach Schedule F 18
19 Unemployment compensation 19
20a Social security benefits . 20a ____ b Taxable amount (see page 24) 20b
21 Other income. List type and amount (see page 24) 21
22 Add the amounts in the far right column for lines 7 through 21. This is your **total income** ▶ 22   **1,378**

Adjusted Gross Income

23 Educator expenses (see page 26) 23
24 Certain business expenses of reservists, performing artists, and fee-basis government officials. Attach Form 2106 or 2106-EZ 24
25 Health savings account deduction. Attach Form 8889 . 25
26 Moving expenses. Attach Form 3903 26
27 One-half of self-employment tax. Attach Schedule SE . 27
28 Self-employed SEP, SIMPLE, and qualified plans . . . 28
29 Self-employed health insurance deduction (see page 26) 29
30 Penalty on early withdrawal of savings 30
31a Alimony paid b Recipient's SSN ▶ ____ 31a
32 IRA deduction (see page 27) 32
33 Student loan interest deduction (see page 30) . . . 33
34 Tuition and fees deduction. Attach Form 8917 34
35 Domestic production activities deduction. Attach Form 8903 35
36 Add lines 23 through 31a and 32 through 35 36
37 Subtract line 36 from line 22. This is your **adjusted gross income** .... ▶ 37   **1,378**

For Disclosure, Privacy Act, and Paperwork Reduction Act Notice, see page 83.   Cat. No. 11320B   Form **1040** (2007)

Taxes and Credits: The section we are now working in is *Tax and Credits.* In general, this section and the next section called *Other Taxes* both relate to taxes owed and credits due. These adjust your amount of income tax due to the federal government. This section talks about things relating to having children, adoption, the elderly and disabled. Since we are assuming you are an unmarried child with no dependents, many of these lines will be blank on your tax return. Let's read each line in order. Use your Form 1040 instructions too.

On the back of the Form 1040, complete Line 38. Line 38 asks to copy the amount from Line 37, Adjusted Gross Income (AGI). This makes things easier as we add and subtract information as we do not have to flip the form back and forth. We are working on the back of the Form 1040 now. Enter $1,378 on Line 38.

Line 39: Answer the questions about being blind. We are assuming you are an unmarried child with no dependents who is not blind. Leave Box 39a blank.

Line 40: *Your Itemized Deductions or Standard Deduction.* You will enter a figure on this line. This line has a little section of instructions on the Form 1040 in the left margin. The first part of those instructions says, "…people who can be claimed as a dependent, see page…in the Form 1040 instructions." This applies to you because your parents will claim you as a dependent. So, let's go to the referenced page in the current Form 1040 instructions.

(Remember how I mentioned about the skill to jump around from one section to another. Here we go!)

On the referenced page of the Form 1040 instructions you find the *Standard Deduction Worksheet for Dependents.* The very first thing it says is to use this worksheet if someone can claim you as a dependent. That is you. Your parents are claiming you as a dependent.

Standard Deduction Worksheet for Dependents—Line 40   *Keep for Your Records*

Use this worksheet **only** if someone can claim you, or your spouse if filing jointly, as a dependent.

1. Is your **earned income*** more than $550?
    ☐ **Yes.** Add $300 to your earned income. Enter the total
    ☐ **No.** Enter $850 } .... 1. _____

2. Enter the amount shown below for your filing status.
    • Single or married filing separately—$5,350
    • Married filing jointly—$10,700 } .... 2. _____
    • Head of household—$7,850

3. **Standard deduction.**
    a. Enter the **smaller** of line 1 or line 2. If born after January 1, 1943, and not blind, **stop here** and enter this amount on Form 1040, line 40. Otherwise, go to line 3b .... **3a.** _____
    b. If born before January 2, 1943, or blind, multiply the number on Form 1040, line 39a, by $1,050 ($1,300 if single or head of household) .... **3b.** _____
    c. Add lines 3a and 3b. Enter the total here and on Form 1040, line 40..................... **3c.** _____

* **Earned income** includes wages, salaries, tips, professional fees, and other compensation received for personal services you performed. It also includes any amount received as a scholarship that you must include in your income. Generally, your earned income is the total of the amount(s) you reported on Form 1040, lines 7, 12, and 18, minus the amount, if any, on line 27.

Note: The income limits change each year so this worksheet will look different each year. Tax year 2007 will not have the exact same figures as the worksheet for 2008 and so on. In other words, when you open the Form 1040 instructions for each year, the questions will be very similar but with different figures and different amounts. When doing real taxes, always use the worksheet in a current Form 1040 instruction booklet, *not* the illustration in this book.

Let's read carefully and answer the questions. You can do this. If you are smart enough to work, you are smart enough to complete this form! Let's complete the 2007 worksheet together using our example figures.

- Line 1: For the first question, "Is your earned income more than $550?" Look at your Form W-2 image from earlier, which says in Box 1 that your wages were $1,370, so put an "X" in the Yes box on the worksheet. Next to the Yes box, it says to add $300 to your earned income and enter the total. So add $300 + $1,370 and write $1,670 in Block number 1 on the right column of the worksheet.

- Line 2: "Enter the amount shown below for your filing status." You know you are single and it says the single amount is $5,350, so write $5,350 on Line 2 on the right column of the worksheet.

- Line 3: Read the text about *Standard Deduction*. Enter the smaller of Line 1 or Line 2. Line 1, $1,670 is smaller than Line 2, $5,350 so write $1,670 on Line 3a. Now, finish reading Line 3, "If born after January 1, 1942 and not blind, stop here and enter this amount on Form 1040, Line 40." That's you! You were born after 1942. You are not blind. Enter $1,670 from Line 3a of the worksheet onto your Form 1040 Line 40.

(Note: The minimum standard deduction you would ever have is $850 for tax year 2007. This is used when you have annual income under $550.) Your completed *Standard Deduction Worksheet* should look like this:

Standard Deduction Worksheet for Dependents—Line 40		*Keep for Your Records*
Use this worksheet **only** if someone can claim you, or your spouse if filing jointly, as a dependent.		
1. Is your **earned income*** more than $550? ☒ **Yes.** Add $300 to your earned income. Enter the total ☐ **No.** Enter $850	.... **1.**	**1,670**
2. Enter the amount shown below for your filing status. • Single or married filing separately—$5,350 • Married filing jointly—$10,700 • Head of household—$7,850	.... **2.**	**5,350**
3. **Standard deduction.** **a.** Enter the **smaller** of line 1 or line 2. If born after January 1, 1943, and not blind, **stop here** and enter this amount on Form 1040, line 40. Otherwise, go to line 3b .... **3a.**		**1,670**
b. If born before January 2, 1943, or blind, multiply the number on Form 1040, line 39a, by $1,050 ($1,300 if single or head of household) .... **3b.**		
c. Add lines 3a and 3b. Enter the total here and on Form 1040, line 40. .... **3c.**		
* Earned income includes wages, salaries, tips, professional fees, and other compensation received for personal services you performed. It also includes any amount received as a scholarship that you must include in your income. Generally, your earned income is the total of the amount(s) you reported on Form 1040, lines 7, 12, and 18, minus the amount, if any, on line 27.		

Now, we are completing the Form 1040 again.

Line 41 is mathematical subtraction. We subtract $1,670 from $1,378 and write -$292 on Line 41. Oh, but it is negative number. Is this ok? Yes it is fine. Write -$292 on Line 41.

Line 42 deals with the number of exemptions you will claim. Ignore the first sentence because Line 38 is not over $112,875.

Let's discuss exemptions. Remember on the front of the form, we had the *Exemptions* section about dependents and if your parents would be claiming you? We determined that you would not have any exemptions. We entered 0 in box 6d on the front of the Form 1040.

You are allowed a $3,200 deduction for each exemption but you have no exemptions so $3,200 multiplied by zero equals zero. You will enter 0 on Line 42.

Line 43, the next line, is mathematical subtraction. When we subtract, we again arrive at -$292, a negative number but this time, the form instructs us to enter 0 if we have a negative number. Write 0 on Line 43.

Line 43 is the amount of income the federal government will tax you on. Yes, that is correct. The amount is 0. Based on the rules, your taxable income has been reduced to zero. (This is one of the benefits of working as a child. Many times your income that is actually taxed will end up being zero.)

Line 44: We would normally look up the tax if you had taxable income on Line 43, but since you do not, we can just enter 0 for the tax amount. (If you had taxable income, there is a chart in your 1040 instructions to tell you the amount to write on the line.)

How to Read and Use a Tax Table

When you do have taxable income on Line 43, you will go to the back of the Form 1040 Instruction booklet and find the Tax Table. The table is set up by income ranges. First locate the line where your income falls. For example, if your taxable income was $1,110 for the year, you would look up the tax listed for the line that reads $1,000 through $1,125. Along this income line, will be the tax for a single person. You would copy this tax amount onto Line 44.

Next, Line 45, *Alternative Minimum Tax* applies to people with very high salaries. We are assuming you have lower income so this line will not apply to you. Leave it blank.

Line 46 tells us to add, and we write 0 on Line 46.

Lines 47 through 55 are all credits that do not apply to dependent children under 18 with no dependents of their own, so you can go straight to Line 56 and enter 0.

Line 57 is math, write 0.

Other Taxes: Lines 58 to 62 are not applicable to children in an Employer—Employee type job so leave these lines all blank.

Line 63 is math again. We write 0.

Payments: Line 64 asks for Federal Income Tax withheld. Copy Box 2 from the Form W-2 example image onto Line 64. Write $137 on Line 64.

Lines 65 through 71 are not applicable to children with lower income so leave them all blank.

There are two credits you may receive in your future called the *Savers Credit* and the *Earned Income Credit*. If you qualify, they both mean more money for you. In both cases, you *must file* a tax return to receive them. (We mention them here to once again emphasize the importance of filing a tax

In your future: *The Savers Credit*

Form 1040 Line 53: At age 18, you *may* qualify for the Retirement Contributions Credit or *savers credit*. If you contributed to an IRA, this nonrefundable credit can be up to $1,000.

You must file your taxes, meet all qualifications, and have taxable income on Line 43 of your Form 1040.

In your future: *Earned Income Tax Credit*

Form 1040 Line 66: Once you turn 25 years old, you *may* qualify for the "earned income credit." In 2007 the maximum refundable credit amount was $4,716!

You must file your taxes and meet qualifications. You do *not* have to have taxable income to receive this credit.

return each year.)

Line 72, *Total Payments*, is adding, and we write $137.

Pause here to be sure you understand this section. This is how much tax was paid to the IRS. We are reporting you paid $137 tax to the IRS. This is true because your employer took it out of your paycheck and reported it on your Form W-2. But if you recall, we showed above that you actually have no taxable income. So what do we expect? We expect a refund!

On Line 73, we do math again and enter $137.

On Line 74a, enter the amount from Line 73 so you will receive all of your money back from the IRS.

Next, enter your routing number for your bank. (You may have to call your bank to find this out.) Then check the savings box and enter your savings account number so they can electronically send the money straight to your account.

Go down to the signature line to sign and date. If you are a full time student write Student for your occupation. Make a photocopy of the Form 1040 for your records. Staple your Form W-2 (copy B) to the front of your return (next to the word *Income* where it says "attach Forms W-2 here"). Add a stamp to the envelope, and mail in your return. If you do not send it in, you will not receive your refund money back. You are finished. You just did a tax return!

How do you know how much you are allowed to contribute to your Roth IRA? Line 7 of your Form 1040 has the amount of your wages or earned income. This is the amount you will compare with the limit for the year and choose which ever figure is *less*. In this example for 2007, Line 7 was $1,370. The maximum allowed is $4,000 (for year 2007) or your earned income, which ever is less. $1,370 is less than $4,000 so you cannot contribute more than $1,370 to an IRA.

The back of your completed Form 1040 should look like this:

Tax and Credits	38	Amount from line 37 (adjusted gross income)	38	**1,378**
	39a	Check { You were born before January 2, 1943, Blind. } Total boxes		
		if: { Spouse was born before January 2, 1943, Blind. } checked ▶ 39a		
Standard Deduction for—	b	If your spouse itemizes on a separate return or you were a dual-status alien, see page 31 and check here ▶39b		
	40	**Itemized deductions** (from Schedule A) or your **standard deduction** (see left margin) .	40	**1,670**
• People who checked any box on line 39a or 39b **or** who can be claimed as a dependent, see page 31.	41	Subtract line 40 from line 38	41	**-292**
	42	If line 38 is $117,300 or less, multiply $3,400 by the total number of exemptions claimed on line 6d. If line 38 is over $117,300, see the worksheet on page 33	42	**0**
	43	**Taxable income.** Subtract line 42 from line 41. If line 42 is more than line 41, enter -0- .	43	**0**
• All others:	44	Tax (see page 33). Check if any tax is from: a Form(s) 8814 b Form 4972 c Form(s) 8889	44	**0**
Single or Married filing separately, $5,350	45	**Alternative minimum tax** (see page 36). Attach Form 6251	45	
	46	Add lines 44 and 45 . . . . ▶	46	**0**
Married filing jointly or Qualifying widow(er), $10,700	47	Credit for child and dependent care expenses. Attach Form 2441	47	
	48	Credit for the elderly or the disabled. Attach Schedule R .	48	
	49	Education credits. Attach Form 8863	49	
Head of household, $7,850	50	Residential energy credits. Attach Form 5695	50	
	51	Foreign tax credit. Attach Form 1116 if required . . .	51	
	52	Child tax credit (see page 39). Attach Form 8901 if required	52	
	53	Retirement savings contributions credit. Attach Form 8880 .	53	
	54	Credits from: a Form 8396 b Form 8859 c Form 8839	54	
	55	Other credits: a Form 3800 b Form 8801 c Form _____	55	
	56	Add lines 47 through 55. These are your **total credits**	56	**0**
	57	Subtract line 56 from line 46. If line 56 is more than line 46, enter -0- . . . . . ▶	57	**0**
Other Taxes	58	Self-employment tax. Attach Schedule SE	58	
	59	Unreported social security and Medicare tax from: a Form 4137 b Form 8919	59	
	60	Additional tax on IRAs, other qualified retirement plans, etc. Attach Form 5329 if required .	60	
	61	Advance earned income credit payments from Form(s) W-2, box 9	61	
	62	Household employment taxes. Attach Schedule H	62	
	63	Add lines 57 through 62. This is your **total tax** . . . . ▶	63	**0**
Payments	64	Federal income tax withheld from Forms W-2 and 1099 .	64	**137**
	65	2007 estimated tax payments and amount applied from 2006 return	65	
If you have a qualifying child, attach Schedule EIC.	66a	Earned income credit (EIC)	66a	
	b	Nontaxable combat pay election ▶	66b	
	67	Excess social security and tier 1 RRTA tax withheld (see page 59)	67	
	68	Additional child tax credit. Attach Form 8812	68	
	69	Amount paid with request for extension to file (see page 59)	69	
	70	Payments from: a Form 2439 b Form 4136 c Form 8885	70	
	71	Refundable credit for prior year minimum tax from Form 8801, line 27	71	
	72	Add lines 64, 65, 66a, and 67 through 71. These are your **total payments** . . . . ▶	72	**137**
Refund	73	If line 72 is more than line 63, subtract line 63 from line 72. This is the amount you **overpaid**	73	**137**
Direct deposit? See page 59 and fill in 74b, 74c, and 74d, or Form 8888.	74a	Amount of line 73 you want **refunded to you.** If Form 8888 is attached, check here ▶	74a	**137**
	▶ b	Routing number **BANK # HERE** ▶ c Type: Checking ☒ Savings		
	▶ d	Account number **YOUR ACCOUNT # HERE**		
	75	Amount of line 73 you want **applied to your 2008 estimated tax** ▶	75	
Amount You Owe	76	**Amount you owe.** Subtract line 72 from line 63. For details on how to pay, see page 60 ▶	76	
	77	Estimated tax penalty (see page 61)	77	
Third Party Designee		Do you want to allow another person to discuss this return with the IRS (see page 61)? Yes. Complete the following. No		
		Designee's name ▶ Phone no. ▶ ( ) Personal identification number (PIN) ▶		

Sign Here
Joint return? See page 13.
Keep a copy for your records.

Under penalties of perjury, I declare that I have examined this return and accompanying schedules and statements, and to the best of my knowledge and belief, they are true, correct, and complete. Declaration of preparer (other than taxpayer) is based on all information of which preparer has any knowledge.

Your signature	Date	Your occupation	Daytime phone number
YOUR SIGNATURE	**DATE**	**STUDENT**	**YOUR PHONE**
Spouse's signature. If a joint return, **both** must sign.	Date	Spouse's occupation	

Paid Preparer's Use Only

Preparer's signature ▶		Date	Check if self-employed	Preparer's SSN or PTIN
Firm's name (or yours if self-employed), address, and ZIP code ▶			EIN	
			Phone no. ( )	

You can use this example year after year to complete your taxes. Just go slowly, step by step, being sure to read carefully when you are told to add or subtract lines.

Tax Return Checklist for an Employee — Employer Job

- Complete Form 1040 personal information
- Answer presidential election campaign question
- Answer filing status question
- Enter interest income from savings account
- Enter income amount for wages (see Form W-2)
- Use the *Standard Deduction Worksheet for Dependents* (see 1040 instructions) to compute your deduction amount
- If needed, look up the tax on your taxable income
- Enter Federal Income Tax withheld (see Form W-2)
- Do the math to see if you have a refund or taxes due
- Review Roth IRA contributions for the year
- Update your Roth IRA contribution sheet (see appendix)
- Complete state and local taxes with a parent's help

IRS Publications that May Help with Tax Returns for Children in an Employee — Employer Job

- Form 1040 *U.S. Individual Income Tax Return Instructions*
- Publication 501, *Exemptions, Standard Deduction and Filing Information*
- Publication 531, *Recording Tip Income*
- Publication 590, *Individual Retirement Arrangements*
- Publication 929, *Tax Rules for Children and Dependents*

Taxes for Job Type 2: Employed in Your Parent's Business

(Tax instructions build on previous tax instructions, so please read prior sections before continuing here.)

Suppose you work for your parents, who own their own business. When you work for your self-employed parents, you are going to receive a Form W-2, just like children employed in an Employer — Employee job type relationship. Let's see what is different.

> (Just a reminder: parents should read our chapter on how to provide a Form W-2 for children.)

Parents, did you know?

By employing your child in your business, you create payroll, a business expense that reduces your business income, which reduces your taxes.

In some cases (depending on your business income) the amount you save in taxes will be equivalent to or more than the amount you have paid your child. If your child invests this pay in an IRA, in a sense, you have diverted your tax dollars into an IRA account for your child!

At the end of the year, you received your Form W-2 from your employer, which is actually Mom or Dad or might be both. This means, it is time to do your taxes. You are going to follow the same rules as those children in an Employer — Employee job relationship.

To show a really good comparison, let's pretend your family owns the pizza restaurant we used in our prior Employer — Employee example. You tax return will be very similar. The only difference is now you work for your family's restaurant. You are now a family employee.

In the case of family employees, I recommended, if you qualified, to write "*Exempt*" on your Form W-4. (See the Form W-4 section.) This makes life much easier for your parents. Because you wrote "*Exempt*" on your Form W-4, you will have no Federal Income Tax withheld and because you are a family employee under age 18, you have no Social Security or Medicare tax withheld. Thus, you receive more money.

> **Example:** You worked at Pete's Pizza in 2007, which is a sole proprietorship owned by your dad, Pete. You claimed "Exempt" on your Form W-4. You did not spend any of your money but deposited every paycheck into you savings account. Your savings account earned $8.32 in interest. In January, your boss, Dad, gives you a Form W-2 that has these entries:

1 Wages, tips, other compensation	2 Federal income tax withheld
1,370.36	0.00
3 Social security wages	4 Social security tax withheld
0.00	0.00
5 Medicare wages and tips	6 Medicare tax withheld
0.00	0.00

Let's do your taxes. You have your Form W-2. You also received $8.32 in interest from your bank savings account (similar to the earlier example). You have your Form 1040 instruction book that you picked up at your local library, which has the Form 1040 inside.

Take out the Form 1040 and proceed as we did in the last scenario for the entire first side of the Form 1040 all the way down to Line 37. (If needed, refer back to the previous section and also use the Form 1040 instructions.)

What do you have on Line 37? Is it $1,378? It should be. Nothing was different so far. You should have $1,370 on Line 7 for your wages and $8 on Line 8a for the amount of your interest. Add those together and you will have $1,378 on Line 22 and on Line 37.

Your completed Form 1040 front side should look like this:

Form 1040 — Department of the Treasury—Internal Revenue Service
U.S. Individual Income Tax Return **2007** IRS Use Only—Do not write or staple in this space.

For the year Jan. 1-Dec. 31, 2007, or other tax year beginning , 2007, ending , 20 | OMB No. 1545-0074

Label
(See instructions on page 12.)
Use the IRS label.
Otherwise, please print or type.

Your first name and initial **YOUR FIRST NAME** Last name **YOUR LAST NAME** | Your social security number **YOUR # HERE**

If a joint return, spouse's first name and initial Last name | Spouse's social security number

Home address (number and street). If you have a P.O. box, see page 12. **YOUR STREET ADDRESS** Apt. no. | ▲ You **must** enter your SSN(s) above. ▲

City, town or post office, state, and ZIP code. If you have a foreign address, see page 12. **YOUR CITY, YOUR STATE YOUR ZIP CODE**

Presidential Election Campaign ▶ Check here if you, or your spouse if filing jointly, want $3 to go to this fund (see page 12) ▶ [X] You [ ] Spouse

Checking a box below will not change your tax or refund.

Filing Status
Check only one box.

1 [X] Single
2 [ ] Married filing jointly (even if only one had income)
3 [ ] Married filing separately. Enter spouse's SSN above and full name here. ▶
4 [ ] Head of household (with qualifying person). (See page 13.) If the qualifying person is a child but not your dependent, enter this child's name here. ▶
5 [ ] Qualifying widow(er) with dependent child (see page 14)

Exemptions

6a [ ] **Yourself.** If someone can claim you as a dependent, **do not** check box 6a
b [ ] **Spouse**

Boxes checked on 6a and 6b ____
No. of children on 6c who:
• lived with you ____
• did not live with you due to divorce or separation (see page 18) ____
Dependents on 6c not entered above ____

c **Dependents:**
(1) First name Last name	(2) Dependent's social security number	(3) Dependent's relationship to you	(4)✓ if qualifying child for child tax credit (see page 15)
			[ ]
			[ ]
			[ ]
			[ ]

If more than four dependents, see page 15.

d Total number of exemptions claimed | Add numbers on lines above ▶ **0**

Income

Attach Form(s) W-2 here. Also attach Forms W-2G and 1099-R if tax was withheld.

If you did not get a W-2, see page 19.

Enclose, but do not attach, any payment. Also, please use Form 1040-V.

7	Wages, salaries, tips, etc. Attach Form(s) W-2	**7** **1,370**
8a	Taxable interest. Attach Schedule B if required	**8a** **8**
b	Tax-exempt interest. **Do not** include on line 8a . . **8b**	
9a	Ordinary dividends. Attach Schedule B if required	**9a**
b	Qualified dividends (see page 19) . . . **9b**	
10	Taxable refunds, credits, or offsets of state and local income taxes (see page 20) . .	**10**
11	Alimony received	**11**
12	Business income or (loss). Attach Schedule C or C-EZ	**12**
13	Capital gain or (loss). Attach Schedule D if required. If not required, check here ▶ [ ]	**13**
14	Other gains or (losses). Attach Form 4797	**14**
15a	IRA distributions . . **15a** b Taxable amount (see page 21)	**15b**
16a	Pensions and annuities **16a** b Taxable amount (see page 22)	**16b**
17	Rental real estate, royalties, partnerships, S corporations, trusts, etc. Attach Schedule E	**17**
18	Farm income or (loss). Attach Schedule F	**18**
19	Unemployment compensation	**19**
20a	Social security benefits . **20a** b Taxable amount (see page 24)	**20b**
21	Other income. List type and amount (see page 24)	**21**
22	Add the amounts in the far right column for lines 7 through 21. This is your **total income** ▶	**22** **1,378**

Adjusted Gross Income

23	Educator expenses (see page 26) **23**	
24	Certain business expenses of reservists, performing artists, and fee-basis government officials. Attach Form 2106 or 2106-EZ **24**	
25	Health savings account deduction. Attach Form 8889 . **25**	
26	Moving expenses. Attach Form 3903 . . . . **26**	
27	One-half of self-employment tax. Attach Schedule SE . **27**	
28	Self-employed SEP, SIMPLE, and qualified plans . . **28**	
29	Self-employed health insurance deduction (see page 26) **29**	
30	Penalty on early withdrawal of savings **30**	
31a	Alimony paid b Recipient's SSN ▶ **31a**	
32	IRA deduction (see page 27) **32**	
33	Student loan interest deduction (see page 30) . . . **33**	
34	Tuition and fees deduction. Attach Form 8917 . . . **34**	
35	Domestic production activities deduction. Attach Form 8903 **35**	
36	Add lines 23 through 31a and 32 through 35	**36**
37	Subtract line 36 from line 22. This is your **adjusted gross income** . . . . ▶	**37** **1,378**

For Disclosure, Privacy Act, and Paperwork Reduction Act Notice, see page 83. Cat. No. 11320B Form **1040** (2007)

So far the form is the same as the last section. Let's turn the form over and write $1,378 on Line 38.

Keep going now all the way to Line 63. (Use the previous instructions and Form 1040 instructions if you need help.) What do you have on Line 63? Was anything different? No, so you should have 0 on Line 63.

Line 64: Let's look at Line 64 which is the Federal Income Tax withheld. Look on your Form W-2 and enter the amount from Box 2. This is the same rule we followed previously, except now you will be entering 0 because nothing was withheld.

Pause here to be sure you understand this line. This is how much tax was paid to the IRS. We are reporting you paid nothing to the IRS. This is true because your dad did not withhold anything from your paycheck since you claimed *Exempt* on your Form W-4.

Line 72 will be math and you will write 0 and for Line 73 you arrive at 0 for the refund amount.

Wait! Why? How come in the last scenario, working as a non-family member you received a nice refund?

Well last time, you received a refund based on what your employer withheld. This time too, you were refunded based on what your employer withheld. The same rule was followed, except this time the amount was 0 because nothing was withheld.

On Line 74a, write 0 and leave all the bank information blank since you are not receiving any refund.

Go down to the signature line to sign, date, enter Student for occupation, and add your phone number. Make a photocopy of the Form 1040 for your records. Staple your Form W-2 (copy B) to the front of your return (next to the word *Income* where it says "attach Forms W-2 here"). Add a stamp to the envelope, and mail in your return. You are finished.

The back of your completed Form 1040 should look like this:

Tax and Credits	38	Amount from line 37 (adjusted gross income)	38	**1,378**
Standard Deduction for—	39a	Check if: ☐ You were born before January 2, 1943, ☐ Blind. ☐ Spouse was born before January 2, 1943, ☐ Blind. Total boxes checked ▶ 39a		
	b	If your spouse itemizes on a separate return or you were a dual-status alien, see page 31 and check here ▶39b ☐		
• People who checked any box on line 39a or 39b or who can be claimed as a dependent, see page 31.	40	Itemized deductions (from Schedule A) or your standard deduction (see left margin)	40	**1,670**
	41	Subtract line 40 from line 38	41	**-292**
	42	If line 38 is $117,300 or less, multiply $3,400 by the total number of exemptions claimed on line 6d. If line 38 is over $117,300, see the worksheet on page 33	42	**0**
	43	Taxable income. Subtract line 42 from line 41. If line 42 is more than line 41, enter -0-	43	**0**
	44	Tax (see page 33). Check if any tax is from: a ☐ Form(s) 8814 b ☐ Form 4972 c ☐ Form(s) 8889	44	**0**
	45	Alternative minimum tax (see page 36). Attach Form 6251	45	
• All others:	46	Add lines 44 and 45 ▶	46	**0**
Single or Married filing separately, $5,350	47	Credit for child and dependent care expenses. Attach Form 2441	47	
	48	Credit for the elderly or the disabled. Attach Schedule R	48	
Married filing jointly or Qualifying widow(er), $10,700	49	Education credits. Attach Form 8863	49	
	50	Residential energy credits. Attach Form 5695	50	
	51	Foreign tax credit. Attach Form 1116 if required	51	
	52	Child tax credit (see page 39). Attach Form 8901 if required	52	
Head of household, $7,850	53	Retirement savings contributions credit. Attach Form 8880	53	
	54	Credits from: a ☐ Form 8396 b ☐ Form 8859 c ☐ Form 8839	54	
	55	Other credits: a ☐ Form 3800 b ☐ Form 8801 c ☐ Form	55	
	56	Add lines 47 through 55. These are your total credits	56	**0**
	57	Subtract line 56 from line 46. If line 56 is more than line 46, enter -0- ▶	57	**0**
Other Taxes	58	Self-employment tax. Attach Schedule SE	58	
	59	Unreported social security and Medicare tax from: a ☐ Form 4137 b ☐ Form 8919	59	
	60	Additional tax on IRAs, other qualified retirement plans, etc. Attach Form 5329 if required	60	
	61	Advance earned income credit payments from Form(s) W-2, box 9	61	
	62	Household employment taxes. Attach Schedule H	62	
	63	Add lines 57 through 62. This is your total tax ▶	63	**0**
Payments	64	Federal income tax withheld from Forms W-2 and 1099	64	**0**
	65	2007 estimated tax payments and amount applied from 2006 return	65	
If you have a qualifying child, attach Schedule EIC.	66a	Earned income credit (EIC)	66a	
	b	Nontaxable combat pay election ▶ 66b		
	67	Excess social security and tier 1 RRTA tax withheld (see page 59)	67	
	68	Additional child tax credit. Attach Form 8812	68	
	69	Amount paid with request for extension to file (see page 59)	69	
	70	Payments from: a ☐ Form 2439 b ☐ Form 4136 c ☐ Form 8885	70	
	71	Refundable credit for prior year minimum tax from Form 8801, line 27	71	
	72	Add lines 64, 65, 66a, and 67 through 71. These are your total payments ▶	72	**0**
Refund	73	If line 72 is more than line 63, subtract line 63 from line 72. This is the amount you overpaid	73	**0**
Direct deposit? See page 59 and fill in 74b, 74c, and 74d, or Form 8888.	74a	Amount of line 73 you want refunded to you. If Form 8888 is attached, check here ▶ ☐	74a	**0**
	b	Routing number ▶ c Type: ☐ Checking ☐ Savings		
	d	Account number		
	75	Amount of line 73 you want applied to your 2008 estimated tax ▶ 75		
Amount You Owe	76	Amount you owe. Subtract line 72 from line 63. For details on how to pay, see page 60 ▶	76	
	77	Estimated tax penalty (see page 61) 77		

Third Party Designee	Do you want to allow another person to discuss this return with the IRS (see page 61)? ☐ Yes. Complete the following. ☐ No
	Designee's name _____ Phone no. ( ) _____ Personal identification number (PIN) ☐☐☐☐☐

Sign Here
Joint return? See page 13. Keep a copy for your records.

Under penalties of perjury, I declare that I have examined this return and accompanying schedules and statements, and to the best of my knowledge and belief, they are true, correct, and complete. Declaration of preparer (other than taxpayer) is based on all information of which preparer has any knowledge.

Your signature	Date	Your occupation	Daytime phone number
YOUR SIGNATURE	**DATE**	**STUDENT**	**(YOUR PHONE**
Spouse's signature. If a joint return, both must sign.	Date	Spouse's occupation	

Paid Preparer's Use Only

Preparer's signature ▶	Date	Check if self-employed ☐	Preparer's SSN or PTIN
Firm's name (or yours if self-employed), address, and ZIP code ▶		EIN	
		Phone no. ( )	

Form **1040** (2007)

You can use this example year after year to complete your taxes. Just go slowly, step by step, being sure to read carefully when you are told to add or subtract lines.

You may ask me, "But if we did not owe any taxes and we are not getting any refund because nothing was withheld, why are we filing?"

The answer is to be sure you are not overlooking a refund, to have good financial records, to have a good work history, and to have back up documentation for your Roth IRA. You now have proof of earned income if anyone were to ask.

Some will say they would not bother to file. But since you can do it yourself and it only costs you a little time, along with postage, why not file? It certainly can't hurt and will save a lot of trouble if at age 65 you need to explain what kind of work you did at age 13.

So, I recommend always filing your taxes. It's a good habit, it's a good experience, and it prepares you for the future. If you keep working for your family, soon you will earn enough income where you will owe taxes. It is just a matter of time. By the time you do owe taxes, you will have enough experience that filing taxes will be fairly easy for you!

How do you know how much you are allowed to contribute to your Roth IRA? Line 7 of your Form 1040 has the amount of your wages or earned income. This is the amount you will compare with the limit for the year and choose which ever figure is *less*. In this example for 2007, Line 7 was $1,370. The maximum allowed is $4,000 (for year 2007) or your earned income, which ever is less. $1,370 is less than $4,000 so you cannot contribute more than $1,370 to an IRA.

Tax Return Checklist for Children Employed by their Self-Employed Parents

- Complete Form 1040 personal information
- Answer presidential election campaign question
- Answer filing status question
- Enter interest income from savings account
- Enter income amount for wages (see Form W-2)
- Use the *Standard Deduction Worksheet for Dependents* (see 1040 instructions) to compute your deduction amount
- If needed, look up the tax on your taxable income
- Enter Federal Income Tax withheld (see Form W-2)
- Do the math to see if you have a refund or taxes due
- Review Roth IRA contributions for the year
- Update your Roth IRA contribution sheet (see appendix)
- Complete state and local taxes with a parent's help

IRS Publications that May Help with Tax Returns for Children Employed by their Self-Employed Parents

- Form 1040 *U.S. Individual Income Tax Return Instructions*
- Form W-4 *Employee's Withholding Allowance Certificate*
- Form W-2 *Instructions for Forms W-2 and W-3, Wage and Tax Statement & Transmittal of Wage and Tax Statements*
- Publication 15 (Circular E) *Employer's Tax Guide*
- Publication 15-A *Employer's Supplemental Tax Guide*
- Publication 334, *Tax Guide for Small Businesses*
- Publication 535, *Business Expenses*
- Publication 583, *Starting a Business & Keeping Records*
- Publication 590, *Individual Retirement Arrangements*
- Publication 929, *Tax Rules for Children and Dependents*

Taxes for Job Type 3: Household Employee for Your Parents

(Tax instructions build on previous tax instructions, so please read prior sections before continuing here.)

So, you work for your parents as a household employee. Maybe you do house cleaning. Maybe you mow the lawn twice a month. What does this mean come tax time? You are very similar to children who work for self-employed parents.

(Just a reminder: parents should read our chapter on how to provide a Form W-2 for children.)

You received your Form W-2 from your employer, which is actually Mom or Dad or might be both. This means it is time to do your taxes. You are going to follow the same rules as those children in an Employer — Employee job relationship.

To show a good comparison, let's pretend your family paid you the exact same amount as the previous scenarios. If you read those sections, some information will be very familiar because it is exactly the same. As a household employee, you work for your family so you are a type of family employee.

In the case of family employees, I recommended to write "*Exempt*" on your Form W-4 if you qualified. (See the Form W-4 Section.) This makes life much easier for your parents. Because you wrote "*Exempt*" on your Form W-4, you will have no Federal Income Tax withheld and because you are a family household employee under age 21, you will also have no Social Security or Medicare tax withheld. This means you are able to keep more of your money for yourself. (In addition, your parents will not need to complete a Schedule H, Household Employment tax form because you are under age 21.)[24]

---

[24] Line A, *Schedule H Instructions, Household Employment Taxes*

Example: In 2007, you mowed your family's lawn twice a month all summer long so your family did not have to hire help. You did not spend any of your money but deposited every dollar into you savings account. You have a Form 1099-INT from your bank for $8.32 interest earned in your savings account. In January your boss, Dad, gives you a Form W-2 that has these entries:

1 Wages, tips, other compensation	2 Federal income tax withheld
1,370.36	0.00
3 Social security wages	4 Social security tax withheld
0.00	0.00
5 Medicare wages and tips	6 Medicare tax withheld
0.00	0.00

As in the previous scenario, we see as a family household employee claiming *Exempt,* you have the same benefits of no federal, Medicare, or Social Security taxes withheld (because your wages were not considered Social Security or Medicare wages). So again we see a *big* difference when you are a family employee. This means you receive more money.

Parents, did you know?

You will not need to file a Household Employment Taxes Form, Schedule H because you do not count wages paid to children under age 21.

Let's do your taxes. You have your Form 1040 instruction booklet that you picked up at your local library, with the Form 1040 inside. Take out the form and begin at the top.

Complete the entire first side of the form all the way down to line 37. (If you have questions, refer back to the previous scenarios or use the Form 1040 instructions.)

What do you have on line 37? Is it $1,378? It should be. Nothing was different so far. You should have $8 on Line 8a for the interest amount and $1,370 on Line 7 for your wages. Add those together and write $1,378 on Line 37. Your form should look like this:

Form **1040**	Department of the Treasury—Internal Revenue Service **U.S. Individual Income Tax Return** 2007		IRS Use Only---Do not write or staple in this space.

For the year Jan. 1-Dec. 31, 2007, or other tax year beginning , 2007, ending , 20 — OMB No. 1545-0074

Label (See instructions on page 12.) Use the IRS label. Otherwise, please print or type.	L A B E L H E R E	Your first name and initial **YOUR FIRST NAME** Last name **YOUR LAST NAME**	Your social security number **YOUR # HERE**
		If a joint return, spouse's first name and initial Last name	Spouse's social security number
		Home address (number and street). If you have a P.O. box, see page 12. **YOUR STREET ADDRESS** Apt. no.	▲ You **must** enter ▲ your SSN(s) above.
		City, town or post office, state, and ZIP code. If you have a foreign address, see page 12. **YOUR CITY, YOUR STATE YOUR ZIP CODE**	Checking a box below will not change your tax or refund.

Presidential Election Campaign ▶ Check here if you, or your spouse if filing jointly, want $3 to go to this fund (see page 12) ▶ ☒ You ☐ Spouse

Filing Status
Check only one box.

1 ☒ Single
2 ☐ Married filing jointly (even if only one had income)
3 ☐ Married filing separately. Enter spouse's SSN above and full name here. ▶
4 ☐ Head of household (with qualifying person). (See page 13.) If the qualifying person is a child but not your dependent, enter this child's name here. ▶
5 ☐ Qualifying widow(er) with dependent child (see page 14)

Exemptions

6a ☐ **Yourself.** If someone can claim you as a dependent, do not check box 6a
b ☐ **Spouse**

c Dependents:				
(1) First name Last name	(2) Dependent's social security number	(3) Dependent's relationship to you	(4)✓ if qualifying child for child tax credit (see page 15)	

Boxes checked on 6a and 6b
No. of children on 6c who:
• lived with you
• did not live with you due to divorce or separation (see page 16)
Dependents on 6c not entered above

If more than four dependents, see page 15.

Add numbers on lines above ▶ **0**

d Total number of exemptions claimed . . . .

Income

Attach Form(s) W-2 here. Also attach Forms W-2G and 1099-R if tax was withheld.

If you did not get a W-2, see page 19.

Enclose, but do not attach, any payment. Also, please use Form 1040-V.

7	Wages, salaries, tips, etc. Attach Form(s) W-2	7	**1,370**
8a	Taxable interest. Attach Schedule B if required	8a	**8**
b	Tax-exempt interest. Do not include on line 8a . . .	8b		
9a	Ordinary dividends. Attach Schedule B if required	9a	
b	Qualified dividends (see page 19) . . .	9b		
10	Taxable refunds, credits, or offsets of state and local income taxes (see page 20) . .	10	
11	Alimony received	11	
12	Business income or (loss). Attach Schedule C or C-EZ	12	
13	Capital gain or (loss). Attach Schedule D if required. If not required, check here ▶ ☐	13	
14	Other gains or (losses). Attach Form 4797	14	
15a	IRA distributions . . . 15a	b Taxable amount (see page 21)	15b	
16a	Pensions and annuities 16a	b Taxable amount (see page 22)	16b	
17	Rental real estate, royalties, partnerships, S corporations, trusts, etc. Attach Schedule E	17	
18	Farm income or (loss). Attach Schedule F	18	
19	Unemployment compensation	19	
20a	Social security benefits 20a	b Taxable amount (see page 24)	20b	
21	Other income. List type and amount (see page 24)	21	
22	Add the amounts in the far right column for lines 7 through 21. This is your **total income** ▶	22	**1,378**

Adjusted Gross Income

23	Educator expenses (see page 26)	23		
24	Certain business expenses of reservists, performing artists, and fee-basis government officials. Attach Form 2106 or 2106-EZ	24		
25	Health savings account deduction. Attach Form 8889 . .	25		
26	Moving expenses. Attach Form 3903	26		
27	One-half of self-employment tax. Attach Schedule SE . .	27		
28	Self-employed SEP, SIMPLE, and qualified plans . . .	28		
29	Self-employed health insurance deduction (see page 26) .	29		
30	Penalty on early withdrawal of savings	30		
31a	Alimony paid b Recipient's SSN ▶	31a		
32	IRA deduction (see page 27)	32		
33	Student loan interest deduction (see page 30)	33		
34	Tuition and fees deduction. Attach Form 8917	34		
35	Domestic production activities deduction. Attach Form 8903	35		
36	Add lines 23 through 31a and 32 through 35	36		
37	Subtract line 36 from line 22. This is your **adjusted gross income** . . . . . ▶	37	**1,378**

For Disclosure, Privacy Act, and Paperwork Reduction Act Notice, see page 83. Cat. No. 11320B Form **1040** (2007)

Turn the form over and write $1,378 on Line 38.

Use the previous two sections instructions along with your Form 1040 instructions, and complete the Form 1040.

Tax and Credits	38	Amount from line 37 (adjusted gross income)	38	**1,378**
	39a	Check if: ☐ You were born before January 2, 1943, ☐ Blind. ☐ Spouse was born before January 2, 1943, ☐ Blind. Total boxes checked ▶ 39a		
Standard Deduction for—	b	If your spouse itemizes on a separate return or you were a dual-status alien, see page 31 and check here ▶39b ☐		
	40	Itemized deductions (from Schedule A) **or** your **standard deduction** (see left margin)	40	**1,670**
	41	Subtract line 40 from line 38	41	**-292**
• People who checked any box on line 39a or 39b or who can be claimed as a dependent, see page 31.	42	If line 38 is $117,300 or less, multiply $3,400 by the total number of exemptions claimed on line 6d. If line 38 is over $117,300, see the worksheet on page 33	42	**0**
	43	**Taxable income.** Subtract line 42 from line 41. If line 42 is more than line 41, enter -0-	43	**0**
	44	**Tax** (see page 33). Check if any tax is from: a ☐ Form(s) 8814 b ☐ Form 4972 c ☐ Form(s) 8889	44	**0**
	45	**Alternative minimum tax** (see page 36). Attach Form 6251	45	
• All others:	46	Add lines 44 and 45 ▶	46	**0**
Single or Married filing separately, $5,350	47	Credit for child and dependent care expenses. Attach Form 2441	47	
	48	Credit for the elderly or the disabled. Attach Schedule R	48	
	49	Education credits. Attach Form 8863	49	
Married filing jointly or Qualifying widow(er), $10,700	50	Residential energy credits. Attach Form 5695	50	
	51	Foreign tax credit. Attach Form 1116 if required	51	
	52	Child tax credit (see page 39). Attach Form 8901 if required	52	
	53	Retirement savings contributions credit. Attach Form 8880	53	
Head of household, $7,850	54	Credits from: a ☐ Form 8396 b ☐ Form 8859 c ☐ Form 8839	54	
	55	Other credits: a ☐ Form 3800 b ☐ Form 8801 c ☐ Form_____	55	
	56	Add lines 47 through 55. These are your **total credits**	56	**0**
	57	Subtract line 56 from line 46. If line 56 is more than line 46, enter -0- ▶	57	**0**
Other Taxes	58	Self-employment tax. Attach Schedule SE	58	
	59	Unreported social security and Medicare tax from: a ☐ Form 4137 b ☐ Form 8919	59	
	60	Additional tax on IRAs, other qualified retirement plans, etc. Attach Form 5329 if required	60	
	61	Advance earned income credit payments from Form(s) W-2, box 9	61	
	62	Household employment taxes. Attach Schedule H	62	
	63	Add lines 57 through 62. This is your **total tax** ▶	63	**0**
Payments	64	Federal income tax withheld from Forms W-2 and 1099	64	**0**
	65	2007 estimated tax payments and amount applied from 2006 return	65	
If you have a qualifying child, attach Schedule EIC.	66a	Earned income credit (EIC)	66a	
	b	Nontaxable combat pay election ▶ 66b		
	67	Excess social security and tier 1 RRTA withheld (see page 59)	67	
	68	Additional child tax credit. Attach Form 8812	68	
	69	Amount paid with request for extension to file (see page 59)	69	
	70	Payments from: a ☐ Form 2439 b ☐ Form 4136 c ☐ Form 8885	70	
	71	Refundable credit for prior year minimum tax from Form 8801, line 27	71	
	72	Add lines 64, 65, 66a, and 67 through 71. These are your **total payments** ▶	72	**0**
Refund Direct deposit? See page 59 and fill in 74b, 74c, and 74d, or Form 8888.	73	If line 72 is more than line 63, subtract line 63 from line 72. This is the amount you **overpaid**	73	**0**
	74a	Amount of line 73 you want **refunded to you.** If Form 8888 is attached, check here ▶ ☐	74a	**0**
	b	Routing number ▶ c Type: ☐ Checking ☐ Savings		
	d	Account number		
	75	Amount of line 73 you want **applied to your 2008 estimated tax** ▶ 75		
Amount You Owe	76	**Amount you owe.** Subtract line 72 from line 63. For details on how to pay, see page 60 ▶	76	
	77	Estimated tax penalty (see page 61) 77		

Third Party Designee

Do you want to allow another person to discuss this return with the IRS (see page 61)? ☐ **Yes.** Complete the following. ☐ **No**

Designee's name ▶	Phone no. ▶ ( )	Personal identification number (PIN) ▶ [ ]

Sign Here

Joint return? See page 13. Keep a copy for your records.

Under penalties of perjury, I declare that I have examined this return and accompanying schedules and statements, and to the best of my knowledge and belief, they are true, correct, and complete. Declaration of preparer (other than taxpayer) is based on all information of which preparer has any knowledge.

Your signature	Date	Your occupation	Daytime phone number
YOUR SIGNATURE	**DATE**	**STUDENT**	**(YOUR PHONE**
Spouse's signature. If a joint return, **both** must sign.	Date	Spouse's occupation	

Paid Preparer's Use Only

Preparer's signature ▶	Date	Check if self-employed ☐	Preparer's SSN or PTIN
Firm's name (or yours if self-employed), address, and ZIP code ▶		EIN	
		Phone no. ( )	

Form **1040** (2007)

Does this form look exactly like the second scenario? Yes it does. You have no refund because nothing was withheld.

The amounts are exactly the same because we assumed you earned the exact same wages. We did this to show you that working for a parent's business is no different than working for your parents as a household employee. (The types of employment are different for your parents because if they own a business, they can write off your payroll, but for you, nothing is different.)

Go down to the signature line to sign, date, enter Student for occupation and add your phone. Make a photocopy of the Form 1040 for your records. Staple your Form W-2 (copy B) to the front of your return (next to the word *Income* where it says "attach Forms W-2 here"). Add a stamp to the envelope, and mail in your return. You are finished.

You can use this example year after year to complete your taxes. Just go slowly, step by step, being sure to read carefully when you are told to add or subtract lines.

Why did you file a return even though you did not owe any taxes and you are not getting any refund?

The answer is to be sure you are not overlooking a refund, to have good financial records, to have a good work history, and to have back up documentation for your Roth IRA. You now have proof of earned income if anyone were to ask.

How do you know how much you are allowed to contribute to your Roth IRA? Line 7 of your Form 1040 has the amount of your wages or earned income. This is the amount you will compare with the limit for the year and choose which ever figure is *less*. In this example for 2007, Line 7 was $1,370. The maximum allowed is $4,000 (for year 2007) or your earned income, which ever is less. $1,370 is less than $4,000 so you cannot contribute more than $1,370 to an IRA.

Tax Return Checklist for Children Employed as a Household Employee by their Parents

- Complete Form 1040 personal information
- Answer presidential election campaign question
- Answer filing status question
- Enter interest income from savings account
- Enter income amount for wages (see Form W-2)
- Use the *Standard Deduction Worksheet for Dependents* (see 1040 instructions) to compute your deduction amount
- If needed, look up the tax on your taxable income
- Enter Federal Income Tax withheld (see Form W-2)
- Do the math to see if you have a refund or taxes due
- Review Roth IRA contributions for the year
- Update your Roth IRA contribution sheet (see appendix)
- Complete state and local taxes with a parent's help

IRS Publications that May Help with Tax Returns for Children Employed as a Household Employee by Their Parents

- Form 1040 *U.S. Individual Income Tax Return Instructions*
- Form W-4 *Employee's Withholding Allowance Certificate*
- Form W-2 *Instructions for Forms W-2 and W-3, Wage and Tax Statement & Transmittal of Wage and Tax Statements*
- Schedule H, *Household Employment Taxes* instructions
- Publication 15 (Circular E) *Employer's Tax Guide*
- Publication 15-A *Employer's Supplemental Tax Guide*
- Publication 334, *Tax Guide for Small Businesses*
- Publication 535, *Business Expenses*
- Publication 583, *Starting a Business & Keeping Records*
- Publication 590, *Individual Retirement Arrangements*
- Publication 926, *Household Employer's Tax Guide*
- Publication 929, *Tax Rules for Children and Dependents*

Taxes for Job Type 4: Self-Employed Child Providing a Service

(Tax instructions build on previous tax instructions, so please read prior sections before continuing here.)

This book recommends you always file a tax return for any type of earned income but by law you must file a tax return if your net self-employment income is $400 or more for 2007.[25]

You have determined that no one is going to provide you with a Form W-2 at the end of the year but you are working and taking home an income. Your work is something you do with the intention of making a profit. It is not a hobby. You are your own boss because you set your work hours and you decide what work you will do. You are self-employed. Do you create a Form W-2 for yourself? No, you do not.

Let's look at how you will file your taxes when you have no Form W-2. The IRS will have you complete additional forms with your tax return. Besides the Form 1040, you will need:

- Schedule C: Profit or Loss from Business
- Schedule SE: Self-Employment Tax

The *Schedule C* is called *Profit or Loss from Business*. This form is used, as the title indicates, to show if you had a profit or loss from your business this year.

This form is used if your business provides a service like babysitting or lawn mowing. It can also be used if you sell products, like craft items (covered in the next section). First you will complete your Schedule C, and then you will complete your Form 1040 as in prior examples. That is the big difference when you are self-employed. You will complete more forms than someone with an Employer — Employee job.

---

[25] Do I have to file an income tax return?, *IRS Publication 334, Tax Guide for Small Businesses* and *Schedule SE Instructions*

Print a Schedule C at **www.irs.gov** or order the form from the IRS. Images in this book are for quick reference only. Please use a real form with larger print. The front of the 2007 Form Schedule C looks like this:

SCHEDULE C (Form 1040)	**Profit or Loss From Business** (Sole Proprietorship)	OMB No. 1545-0074
Department of the Treasury Internal Revenue Service (99)	▶ Partnerships, joint ventures, etc., must file Form 1065 or 1065-B. ▶ Attach to Form 1040, 1040NR, or 1041. ▶ See Instructions for Schedule C (Form 1040).	**2007** Attachment Sequence No. **09**

Name of proprietor	Social security number (SSN)

A Principal business or profession, including product or service (see page C-2 of the instructions)
B Enter code from pages C-8, 9, & 10 ▶

C Business name. If no separate business name, leave blank.
D Employer ID number (EIN), if any

E Business address (including suite or room no.) ▶
City, town or post office, state, and ZIP code

F Accounting method: (1) ☐ Cash (2) ☐ Accrual (3) ☐ Other (specify) ▶
G Did you "materially participate" in the operation of this business during 2007? If "No," see page C-3 for limit on losses ☐ Yes ☐ No
H If you started or acquired this business during 2007, check here . . . . ▶ ☐

Part I Income

1	Gross receipts or sales. **Caution.** If this income was reported to you on Form W-2 and the "Statutory employee" box on that form was checked, see page C-3 and check here . . . . ▶ ☐	**1**
2	Returns and allowances	**2**
3	Subtract line 2 from line 1	**3**
4	Cost of goods sold (from line 42 on page 2)	**4**
5	**Gross profit.** Subtract line 4 from line 3.	**5**
6	Other income, including federal and state gasoline or fuel tax credit or refund (see page C-3). .	**6**
7	**Gross income.** Add lines 5 and 6 . . . . ▶	**7**

Part II Expenses. Enter expenses for business use of your home **only** on line 30.

8	Advertising	**8**	18	Office expense	**18**
9	Car and truck expenses (see page C-4)	**9**	19	Pension and profit-sharing plans	**19**
			20	Rent or lease (see page C-5):	
10	Commissions and fees . .	**10**	a	Vehicles, machinery, and equipment .	**20a**
11	Contract labor (see page C-4)	**11**	b	Other business property . .	**20b**
12	Depletion	**12**	21	Repairs and maintenance . .	**21**
13	Depreciation and section 179 expense deduction (not included in Part III) (see page C-4)	**13**	22	Supplies (not included in Part III) .	**22**
			23	Taxes and licenses . . .	**23**
			24	Travel, meals, and entertainment:	
14	Employee benefit programs (other than on line 19). .	**14**	a	Travel	**24a**
			b	Deductible meals and entertainment (see page C-6)	**24b**
15	Insurance (other than health) .	**15**	25	Utilities	**25**
16	Interest:		26	Wages (less employment credits) .	**26**
a	Mortgage (paid to banks, etc.)	**16a**	27	Other expenses (from line 48 on page 2)	**27**
b	Other	**16b**			
17	Legal and professional services	**17**			

28	**Total expenses** before expenses for business use of home. Add lines 8 through 27 in columns . ▶	**28**
29	Tentative profit (loss). Subtract line 28 from line 7	**29**
30	Expenses for business use of your home. Attach **Form 8829**	**30**
31	Net profit or (loss). Subtract line 30 from line 29. • If a profit, enter on both **Form 1040, line 12,** and **Schedule SE, line 2,** or on **Form 1040NR, line 13** (statutory employees, see page C-7). Estates and trusts, enter on Form 1041, line 3. • If a loss, you **must** go to line 32.	**31**
32	If you have a loss, check the box that describes your investment in this activity (see page C-7). • If you checked 32a, enter the loss on both **Form 1040, line 12,** and **Schedule SE, line 2,** or on **Form 1040NR, line 13** (statutory employees, see page C-7). Estates and trusts, enter on Form 1041, line 3. • If you checked 32b, you **must** attach **Form 6198.** Your loss may be limited.	**32a** ☐ All investment is at risk. **32b** ☐ Some investment is not at risk.

For Paperwork Reduction Act Notice, see page C-8 of the instructions.	Cat. No. 11334P	Schedule C (Form 1040) 2007

The back of the 2007 Form Schedule C looks like this:

Part III   Cost of Goods Sold (see page C-7)

33   Method(s) used to value closing inventory: **a** ☐ Cost   **b** ☐ Lower of cost or market   **c** ☐ Other (attach explanation)

34   Was there any change in determining quantities, costs, or valuations between opening and closing inventory? If "Yes," attach explanation . . . . ☐ Yes   ☐ No

35 Inventory at beginning of year. If different from last year's closing inventory, attach explanation . .	**35**
36 Purchases less cost of items withdrawn for personal use	**36**
37 Cost of labor. Do not include any amounts paid to yourself	**37**
38 Materials and supplies	**38**
39 Other costs	**39**
40 Add lines 35 through 39	**40**
41 Inventory at end of year	**41**
42 Cost of goods sold. Subtract line 41 from line 40. Enter the result here and on page 1, line 4 . .	**42**

Part IV   Information on Your Vehicle. Complete this part **only** if you are claiming car or truck expenses on line 9 and are not required to file Form 4562 for this business. See the instructions for line 13 on page C-4 to find out if you must file Form 4562.

43   When did you place your vehicle in service for business purposes? (month, day, year) ▶ . . . . / . . . . / . . . .

44   Of the total number of miles you drove your vehicle during 2007, enter the number of miles you used your vehicle for:

a   Business . . . . **b** Commuting (see instructions) . . . . **c** Other . . . .

45   Do you (or your spouse) have another vehicle available for personal use?. . . . . ☐ Yes   ☐ No

46   Was your vehicle available for personal use during off-duty hours? . . . . ☐ Yes   ☐ No

47a   Do you have evidence to support your deduction? . . . . ☐ Yes   ☐ No

   b   If "Yes," is the evidence written? . . . . ☐ Yes   ☐ No

Part V   Other Expenses. List below business expenses not included on lines 8–26 or line 30.

....		
....		
....		
....		
....		
....		
....		
....		
....		

48   Total other expenses. Enter here and on page 1, line 27 . . . .   **48**

✿ *Printed on recycled paper*   Schedule C (Form 1040) 2007

Think of the Schedule C as taking the place of your Form W-2. (You could also have a Form 1099-Misc. See the box below.) Your Schedule C will show the income you earned from your business this year (similar to how a Form W-2 shows the salary you earned from your employer for the year).

Form 1099-Misc

Occasionally children might work for a company on a temporary basis where they are not considered an employee. Instead of a Form W-2, these companies provide a *Non-employee Compensation Form*, the Form 1099-Misc. Income will be listed in Box 7, on the Form 1099-Misc. This type of income is also recorded on a Schedule C. (You would copy the amount you earned from Box 7 of the Form 1099-Misc onto Line 1, *Gross Receipts or Sales* of the Schedule C and then proceed as usual through the Schedule C instructions.)

First we will look at completing a Schedule C for a service business because that is the most popular for self-employed kids. Kids like you are babysitting, mowing lawns, helping the elderly carry in groceries, walking dogs, feeding cats, and more. Kids are selling their time and selling their help. They are providing a service.

> *Example:* You are a babysitter who earned $1,370 in 2007. You spent $25 on a business license. You received $8.32 in interest from your bank savings account.

At the top of the Schedule C is your personal information. The name of the *Proprietor* is your first and last name. Also enter your Social Security number.

Line A, *Principal Business or Profession*: You will enter about 2 to 5 words describing the service you provide. (Babysitting, Dog walking, Lawn Service, etc.)

Line B, *Professional Code:* Enter the code that your job falls under. There is a list of codes in the Schedule C Instructions. Here are some popular principal business codes: [26]

- Lawn Mowing = 561730 for *Selling Landscaping Services*
- Babysitting = 624410 for *Child Day Care Services*
- Dog Walking/Cat Feeding = 812910 for *Pet Care Services*
- Elderly Assistant = 624100 *Individual / Family Services*
- Retail Selling (crafts, etc.) = 453220 *Gift, Novelty, Souvenir Store* (covered in the next section)

Suppose you do all of those things above? Do you need to complete several forms Schedule C? No, if your business does several of those things above, then the business itself is an "odd jobs" business which can fall under code 624100 *Individual Family Services* (assisting families).

For our example, since you are a babysitter, write code 624410 in Block B for *Child Day Care Services*.

Line C, *Business Name*: Leave this blank if you do not have one yet.

Line D will be blank because you do not have an EIN.

Line E, *Business Address:* Write your home address.

Line F, *Accounting Method:* For a service business, where you are just providing a service and have no inventory, you want to choose cash basis accounting.[27] Write an X in the cash method box.

Using the *cash method* means you will record cash when you receive it and record expenses when you spend them. You are already doing this if you are using the *Income* and *Expense*

---

[26] *Schedule C Instructions*
[27] Accounting methods in *IRS Publication 334, Tax Guide for Small Business* and *IRS Publication 538 Accounting Periods and Methods*

sheets explained previously and provided in the appendix of this book. Remember these:

INCOME SHEET For: _____ (write your name and job here)

Date	Time In	Time Out	Task	Location	Hired By: Person & Phone	Amount paid

EXPENSE SHEET – Staple Receipts to the back

Date Incurred	Date Paid	Expense Amount	Expense Description	Expense Category

Line G wants to know if you materially participated in the operation of the business. Check yes because you did. It is your business and no one else works in it but you.

For Line H, check the box if you started your business this year. (In later years, you will leave this box unchecked.)

This is good time to note that every year, you will keep your same business code, same business name if you have one, and same accounting method. If any of these things change, you probably have a new business and you will need to consult a tax advisor.

Part I, Income: As we move on to Part I, we can see that it is going to be about income so we can expect to use our *Income Sheet* paperwork. Now you can see the importance of keeping good records.

Line 1 is *Gross Receipts or Sales*. If you have more than one *Income Sheet*, you would run a total of all the amounts paid to arrive at the total amount you were paid this year and enter this amount on Line 1, *Gross Receipts or Sales*.

In order to see some comparisons with our other employment examples, in our example we said from your babysitting money, your total gross sales were $1,370 (which is the figure we used in the other children's work examples). Let's see what happens and what might be different.

On Line 1, *Gross Receipts* of the Schedule C, enter $1,370.

Line 2 is for *Returns and Allowances*. Remember we are only talking about service business at this point so you have no returns and allowances. There is nothing to return. You provide a service of giving your time and completing a task. Leave this line blank.

Line 3 is a math computation and we subtract Line 2, which is 0, and we write $1,370 on Line 3.

Line 4 refers to *Cost of Goods Sold* but you are not selling any goods, so leave this line blank and move to Line 5 which is math again. Subtracting Line 4 from Line 3 we again enter $1,370 on Line 5.

Line 6 is *Other Income*. Did you receive any other income related to your business besides what was on your *Income Sheet*? Not in our example, so leave this line blank.

Line 7 is math again and is your *Total Gross Income*. Enter $1,370. That's it for income on the Schedule C.

Part II, Expenses: When we discussed self-employment we mentioned obtaining a business license. Our example assumes you paid $25 for your license. (You borrowed from Mom and paid Mom back with some of your babysitting money from your first job.) So you have a license expense. Enter $25 on Line 23, *Taxes and Licenses*.

Now is also a good time to look at the other types of expenses because you may have them in the future. Just take a moment and read through the list in this section. If you buy business cards next year, you would have an *Advertising Expense* because you are buying them to advertise your business. You may have a *Supply Expense* too if you buy a receipt book and begin to give your customers receipts.

Line 28 is the total of all our expenses. Write $25.

Line 29 is math again. Subtract $25 on Line 28 from $1,370 on Line 7 and write $1,345 on Line29. This is your *Net Profit*.

Line 30 deals with using part of your home for your business, for example, a home office. This does not apply to you at this time because you do not pay the mortgage or rent on your home. Leave Line 30 blank.

For Line 31, subtract and we arrive at $1,345 again. Line 31 also tells us to take this amount and enter it on Line 12 of our Form 1040. (Note: It also says to bring this amount to Schedule SE, Line 2. We will complete that form shortly.)

Line 32 concerns a business loss which this book does not address. If you have a loss, consult a tax professional.

That's it for the Schedule C. You are finished with your Schedule C for a service type business.

Flip the form over to see what we did *not* need to complete.

Part III, Cost of Goods Sold: If you were selling a product, you would need to deal with this section.

Part IV, Information on your Vehicle: This is about your vehicle (car or truck) used for business. When you have a car that you use for business (a car that you pay the expenses on), you can keep track of your miles and deduct this as an expense. You would keep track of the miles driven on each trip and multiply it by a standard mileage rate set by the IRS each year. The mileage rate adjusts every year with inflation.

Part V, Other Expenses: If you had expenses that did not fall into one of the categories on the front of the form, you would list them here and then, enter the sum of all these other expenses on the front of the Schedule C on Line 27.

The back of your Schedule C is blank and the front of your completed Schedule C should look like this:

SCHEDULE C (Form 1040)	**Profit or Loss From Business**	OMB No. 1545-0074
Department of the Treasury Internal Revenue Service (99)	(Sole Proprietorship) ► **Partnerships, joint ventures, etc., must file Form 1065 or 1065-B.** ► **Attach to Form 1040, 1040NR, or 1041.** ► **See Instructions for Schedule C (Form 1040).**	20**07** Attachment Sequence No. **09**

Name of proprietor **YOUR FIRST AND LAST NAME HERE**	Social security number (SSN) **YOUR # HERE**

A Principal business or profession, including product or service (see page C-2 of the instructions)
YOUR JOB DESCRIPTION (example: Child Care) **B** Enter code from pages C-8, 9, & 10 ► 6 2 4 4 1 0

C Business name. If no separate business name, leave blank.   **D** Employer ID number (EIN), if any

E Business address (including suite or room no.) ► **YOUR STREET ADDRESS**
City, town or post office, state, and ZIP code   **YOUR CITY, YOUR STATE   ZIPCODE**

F Accounting method: (1) **X** Cash   (2) ☐ Accrual   (3) ☐ Other (specify) ► ....

G Did you "materially participate" in the operation of this business during 2007? If "No," see page C-3 for limit on losses   **X** Yes ☐ No

H If you started or acquired this business during 2007, check here . . . . ► **X**

Part I   Income

1	Gross receipts or sales. **Caution.** If this income was reported to you on Form W-2 and the "Statutory employee" box on that form was checked, see page C-3 and check here . . . . . . ► ☐		**1**	**1,370**
2	Returns and allowances		**2**	**0**
3	Subtract line 2 from line 1		**3**	**1,370**
4	Cost of goods sold (from line 42 on page 2)		**4**	**0**
5	**Gross profit.** Subtract line 4 from line 3		**5**	**1,370**
6	Other income, including federal and state gasoline or fuel tax credit or refund (see page C-3). .		**6**	**0**
7	**Gross income.** Add lines 5 and 6 . . . . ►		**7**	**1,370**

Part II   Expenses. Enter expenses for business use of your home **only** on line 30.

8	Advertising	**8**		18	Office expense	**18**	
9	Car and truck expenses (see page C-4)	**9**		19	Pension and profit-sharing plans	**19**	
10	Commissions and fees .	**10**		20	Rent or lease (see page C-5):		
11	Contract labor (see page C-4)	**11**			a Vehicles, machinery, and equipment .	**20a**	
12	Depletion	**12**			b Other business property . . .	**20b**	
13	Depreciation and section 179 expense deduction (not included in Part III) (see page C-4)	**13**		21	Repairs and maintenance . . .	**21**	
				22	Supplies (not included in Part III) .	**22**	
				23	Taxes and licenses	**23**	**25**
				24	Travel, meals, and entertainment:		
					a Travel	**24a**	
14	Employee benefit programs (other than on line 19). .	**14**			b Deductible meals and entertainment (see page C-6)	**24b**	
15	Insurance (other than health) .	**15**		25	Utilities	**25**	
16	Interest:			26	Wages (less employment credits) .	**26**	
	a Mortgage (paid to banks, etc.) .	**16a**		27	Other expenses (from line 48 on page 2)	**27**	
	b Other	**16b**					
17	Legal and professional services	**17**					

28	**Total expenses** before expenses for business use of home. Add lines 8 through 27 in columns . ►		**28**	**25**
29	Tentative profit (loss). Subtract line 28 from line 7		**29**	**1,345**
30	Expenses for business use of your home. Attach **Form 8829**		**30**	
31	**Net profit or (loss).** Subtract line 30 from line 29. • If a profit, enter on both **Form 1040, line 12,** and **Schedule SE, line 2,** or on **Form 1040NR, line 13** (statutory employees, see page C-7). Estates and trusts, enter on Form 1041, line 3. • If a loss, you **must** go to line 32.	}	**31**	**1,345**
32	If you have a loss, check the box that describes your investment in this activity (see page C-7). • If you checked 32a, enter the loss on both **Form 1040, line 12,** and **Schedule SE, line 2,** or on **Form 1040NR, line 13** (statutory employees, see page C-7). Estates and trusts, enter on Form 1041, line 3. • If you checked 32b, you **must** attach **Form 6198.** Your loss may be limited.	}	32a ☐ All investment is at risk. 32b ☐ Some investment is not at risk.

For Paperwork Reduction Act Notice, see page C-8 of the instructions.	Cat. No. 11334P	Schedule C (Form 1040) 2007

Since your Schedule C is complete, we need to begin the Form 1040. You have your Form 1040 instruction book that you picked up at your local library with the Form 1040 inside.

Begin at the top. Assume you have a Form 1099-INT for $8.32 in interest from your saving account this year. (If needed, use the instructions from the previous sections. You should be fairly comfortable flipping through pages now.) Complete through Line 8a in the *Income* section.

Are you in the *Income* section? Did you enter $8 for interest on Line 8a? We are assuming your savings account paid the same amount of interest as previous examples so you can compare scenarios. Write your $8 in interest on Line 8a.

What did you write for wages on Line 7? If it is blank, you did awesome! It should be blank. You have no Form W-2.

You will notice that you already have an entry on Line 12 of your Form 1040. You entered that when you completed your Schedule C. The IRS provides a separate line to report your business income. (It does not go on Line 7, Wages.)

That's it for your income. You know that because as in our other examples, you know you only had some bank interest and business income and both of those are on your Form 1040. You have accounted for all your income this year.

Add the total income for Line 22. Add your $8 on Line 8a plus your entry of $1,345 on Line 12 to arrive at your total of $1,353 for Line 22, your *Total Income*.

Let's look at *Adjusted Gross Income*. Remember under certain circumstances the government will let you reduce your taxable income and this whole section applies to that. Remember, we said a Traditional IRA would be entered on Line 32, if you had one. Well, you do not have a Traditional IRA but you do have what is called Self-Employment Tax and you are able to deduct half of that amount on Line 27.

Let's see what this is all about. We will use the *Schedule SE, Self-Employment Tax Form* to compute the amount for Line 27. Print a Schedule SE at **www.irs.gov** or order the form from the IRS. Here is what the Form Schedule SE looks like:

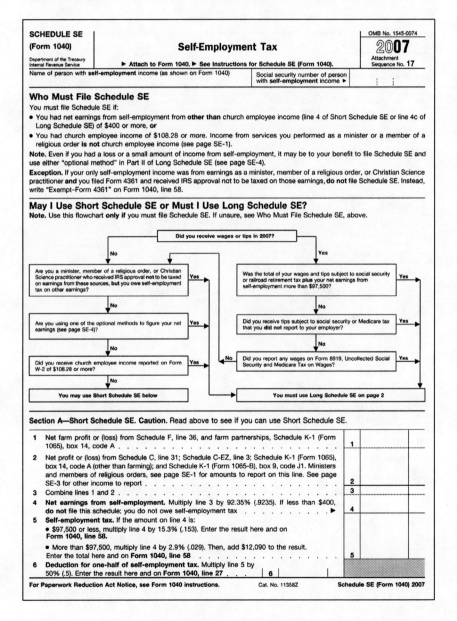

Remember, Images in this book are for quick reference only. Please use a real form with large print. For your information, here is an image of the longer form on the back of the Schedule SE (which you will not need to complete since you have low income).

Schedule SE (Form 1040) 2007	Attachment Sequence No. **17**	Page **2**

Name of person with **self-employment** income (as shown on Form 1040)	Social security number of person with **self-employment** income ▶

Section B—Long Schedule SE

Part I   Self-Employment Tax

Note. If your only income subject to self-employment tax is **church employee income**, skip lines 1 through 4b. Enter -0- on line 4c and go to line 5a. Income from services you performed as a minister or a member of a religious order **is not** church employee income. See page SE-1.

A   If you are a minister, member of a religious order, or Christian Science practitioner **and** you filed Form 4361, but you had $400 or more of **other** net earnings from self-employment, check here and continue with Part I . . . . . ▶ ☐

1	Net farm profit or (loss) from Schedule F, line 36, and farm partnerships, Schedule K-1 (Form 1065), box 14, code A. **Note.** Skip this line if you use the farm optional method (see page SE-4)	**1**	
2	Net profit or (loss) from Schedule C, line 31; Schedule C-EZ, line 3; Schedule K-1 (Form 1065), box 14, code A (other than farming); and Schedule K-1 (Form 1065-B), box 9, code J1. Ministers and members of religious orders, see page SE-1 for amounts to report on this line. See page SE-3 for other income to report. **Note.** Skip this line if you use the nonfarm optional method (see page SE-4)	**2**	
3	Combine lines 1 and 2	**3**	
4a	If line 3 is more than zero, multiply line 3 by 92.35% (.9235). Otherwise, enter amount from line 3	**4a**	
b	If you elect one or both of the optional methods, enter the total of lines 15 and 17 here . . .	**4b**	
c	Combine lines 4a and 4b. If less than $400, **stop;** you do not owe self-employment tax. **Exception.** If less than $400 and you had **church employee income,** enter -0- and continue. . . . . . ▶	**4c**	
5a	Enter your **church employee income** from Form W-2. See page SE-1 for definition of church employee income **5a**		
b	Multiply line 5a by 92.35% (.9235). If less than $100, enter -0-	**5b**	
6	**Net earnings from self-employment.** Add lines 4c and 5b	**6**	
7	Maximum amount of combined wages and self-employment earnings subject to social security tax or the 6.2% portion of the 7.65% railroad retirement (tier 1) tax for 2007	**7**	97,500 00
8a	Total social security wages and tips (total of boxes 3 and 7 on Form(s) W-2) and railroad retirement (tier 1) compensation. If $97,500 or more, skip lines 8b through 10, and go to line 11 . . . . **8a**		
b	Unreported tips subject to social security tax (from Form 4137, line 10) **8b**		
c	Wages subject to social security tax (from Form 8919, line 10) . . . **8c**		
d	Add lines 8a, 8b, and 8c	**8d**	
9	Subtract line 8d from line 7. If zero or less, enter -0- here and on line 10 and go to line 11 . ▶	**9**	
10	Multiply the **smaller** of line 6 or line 9 by 12.4% (.124)	**10**	
11	Multiply line 6 by 2.9% (.029)	**11**	
12	**Self-employment tax.** Add lines 10 and 11. Enter here and on **Form 1040, line 58**	**12**	
13	**Deduction for one-half of self-employment tax.** Multiply line 12 by 50% (.5). Enter the result here and on **Form 1040, line 27** . . . **13**		

Part II   Optional Methods To Figure Net Earnings (see page SE-4)

Farm Optional Method. You may use this method **only if (a)** your gross farm income[1] was not more than $2,400, **or (b)** your net farm profits[2] were less than $1,733.

14	Maximum income for optional methods	**14**	1,600 00
15	Enter the **smaller** of: two-thirds (⅔) of gross farm income[1] (not less than zero) **or** $1,600. Also include this amount on line 4b above	**15**	

Nonfarm Optional Method. You may use this method **only if (a)** your net nonfarm profits[3] were less than $1,733 and also less than 72.189% of your gross nonfarm income,[4] **and (b)** you had net earnings from self-employment of at least $400 in 2 of the prior 3 years.

Caution. You may use this method no more than five times.

16	Subtract line 15 from line 14	**16**	
17	Enter the **smaller** of: two-thirds (⅔) of gross nonfarm income[4] (not less than zero) **or** the amount on line 16. Also include this amount on line 4b above	**17**	

[1] From Sch. F, line 11, and Sch. K-1 (Form 1065), box 14, code B.

[2] From Sch. F, line 36, and Sch. K-1 (Form 1065), box 14, code A.

[3] From Sch. C, line 31; Sch. C-EZ, line 3; Sch. K-1 (Form 1065), box 14, code A; and Sch. K-1 (Form 1065-B), box 9, code J1.

[4] From Sch. C, line 7; Sch. C-EZ, line 1; Sch. K-1 (Form 1065), box 14, code C; and Sch. K-1 (Form 1065-B), box 9, code J2.

Schedule SE (Form 1040) 2007

Remember in our first type of job, you received a Form W-2 for wages and you had both Social Security and Medicare taxes withheld. Well, just because you pay yourself, doesn't mean you are permitted to forget about paying Social Security and Medicare Taxes. You still have to pay into Social Security and Medicare.

However, on Line 27, *One-half of Self-Employment Tax*, you can deduct half of the total amount you pay. That's good news but how much will it be?

We need to compute the amount. (Here is the third form I told you would come.) Let's fill out the Schedule SE. The top of the form has your personal information: name and Social Security number. We are going to assume you have a low amount of income, as in our example and did not receive tips. (If this is not the case, use the long form on side 2 and consult with a tax professional.)

We are completing the short Schedule SE Form.

Line 1: Leave this line blank because it pertains to farms.

Line 2: This amount comes from your Schedule C, Line 31, *Net Profit*, enter $1,345.

Line 3 is math, so add Line 1 + Line 2 and write $1,345.

For Line 4, *Net Earnings from Self-employment*, read and use your calculator. Multiply Line 3 which is $1,345 by 92.35% (.09235) and you arrive at $1,242.

If this amount was less than $400, then we would not file this form, you would not owe self-employment income tax. There is that $400 rule! This means that if your income is low enough, you will not have to pay Social Security and Medicare taxes even though you are self-employed.

Thus, we have now learned the second way to avoid paying Social Security and Medicare taxes. The second way to avoid the taxes is to have net self-employment income under $400. (Remember, the first way you can avoid Social Security and Medicare taxes was if you were under 18 employed in your parents business or a household employee under 21.)

But in our scenario, you did earn more than $400 on Line 4, so you will have to pay taxes. Write $1,242 on Line 4 of your Schedule SE and let's look at Line 5.

For Line 5, *Self-Employment Tax*, we just have to read carefully again. If the amount on Line 4, $1,242, is $94,200 or less (which it is), multiply by 15.3% (.153). $1,242 multiplied by .153 equals $190. Write $190 on Line 5 and also on the back of our Form 1040, Line 58. (Line 5 tells you to do this.)

Section A—Short Schedule SE. Caution. Read above to see if you can use Short Schedule SE.

1	Net farm profit or (loss) from Schedule F, line 36, and farm partnerships, Schedule K-1 (Form 1065), box 14, code A . . .	1	
2	Net profit or (loss) from Schedule C, line 31; Schedule C-EZ, line 3; Schedule K-1 (Form 1065), box 14, code A (other than farming); and Schedule K-1 (Form 1065-B), box 9, code J1. Ministers and members of religious orders, see page SE-1 for amounts to report on this line. See page SE-3 for other income to report	2	**1,345**
3	Combine lines 1 and 2	3	**1,345**
4	**Net earnings from self-employment.** Multiply line 3 by 92.35% (.9235). If less than $400, do not file this schedule; you do not owe self-employment tax . . . . ▶	4	**1,242**
5	**Self-employment tax.** If the amount on line 4 is: • $97,500 or less, multiply line 4 by 15.3% (.153). Enter the result here and on **Form 1040, line 58.** • More than $97,500, multiply line 4 by 2.9% (.029). Then, add $12,090 to the result. Enter the total here and on **Form 1040, line 58**	5	**190**
6	**Deduction for one-half of self-employment tax.** Multiply line 5 by 50% (.5). Enter the result here and on **Form 1040, line 27** . . .	6	

For Paperwork Reduction Act Notice, see Form 1040 Instructions.	Cat. No. 11358Z	Schedule SE (Form 1040) 2007

Ok, so we computed an amount for Line 58 of the Form 1040 but we wanted the amount for Line 27 for the Form 1040! Well Line 27 says, "One half of self-employment tax." If $190 was the full amount, we divide that amount by 2 and write $95 on Form 1040, Line 27.

This is the only adjustment you have to make in the *Adjusted Gross Income* section, so skip down to Line 36 which tells you to add all adjustments. Enter $95 on Line 36.

For Line 37, subtract Line 36, $95 from Line 22, your total income of $1,353 and you arrive at $1,258 as your *Adjusted Gross Income (AGI)*. Write $1,258 on Line 37. Our *AGI* has changed from prior scenarios because we were allowed to deduct both expenses and half Self-Employment taxes.

Copy this amount to the top of the back of the Form 1040, Line 38.

The front of your Form 1040 should look like this:

Form **1040**	Department of the Treasury—Internal Revenue Service **2007** **U.S. Individual Income Tax Return**		IRS Use Only—Do not write or staple in this space.

For the year Jan. 1-Dec. 31, 2007, or other tax year beginning , 2007, ending , 20 | OMB No. 1545-0074

Label
(See instructions on page 12.)
Use the IRS label.
Otherwise, please print or type.

Your first name and initial — **YOUR FIRST NAME** | Last name — **YOUR LAST NAME** | Your social security number — **YOUR # HERE**

If a joint return, spouse's first name and initial | Last name | Spouse's social security number

Home address (number and street). If you have a P.O. box, see page 12. — **YOUR STREET ADDRESS** | Apt. no. | ▲ You **must** enter your SSN(s) above. ▲

City, town or post office, state, and ZIP code. If you have a foreign address, see page 12. — **YOUR CITY, YOUR STATE YOUR ZIP CODE** | Checking a box below will not change your tax or refund.

Presidential Election Campaign ▶ Check here if you, or your spouse if filing jointly, want $3 to go to this fund (see page 12) ▶ [X] You [ ] Spouse

Filing Status
Check only one box.

1 [X] Single
2 [ ] Married filing jointly (even if only one had income)
3 [ ] Married filing separately. Enter spouse's SSN above and full name here. ▶
4 [ ] Head of household (with qualifying person). (See page 13.) If the qualifying person is a child but not your dependent, enter this child's name here. ▶
5 [ ] Qualifying widow(er) with dependent child (see page 14)

Exemptions

6a [ ] **Yourself.** If someone can claim you as a dependent, **do not** check box 6a
b [ ] **Spouse**
c **Dependents:**

(1) First name Last name	(2) Dependent's social security number	(3) Dependent's relationship to you	(4) ✓ if qualifying child for child tax credit (see page 15)
			[ ]
			[ ]
			[ ]
			[ ]

If more than four dependents, see page 15.

Boxes checked on 6a and 6b
No. of children on 6c who:
• lived with you
• did not live with you due to divorce or separation (see page 18)
Dependents on 6c not entered above
Add numbers on lines above ▶ **0**

d Total number of exemptions claimed

Income

Attach Form(s) W-2 here. Also attach Forms W-2G and 1099-R if tax was withheld.

If you did not get a W-2, see page 19.

Enclose, but do not attach, any payment. Also, please use Form 1040-V.

7	Wages, salaries, tips, etc. Attach Form(s) W-2	7	
8a	Taxable interest. Attach Schedule B if required	8a	8
b	Tax-exempt interest. Do not include on line 8a	8b	
9a	Ordinary dividends. Attach Schedule B if required	9a	
b	Qualified dividends (see page 19)	9b	
10	Taxable refunds, credits, or offsets of state and local income taxes (see page 20)	10	
11	Alimony received	11	
12	Business income or (loss). Attach Schedule C or C-EZ	12	1,345
13	Capital gain or (loss). Attach Schedule D if required. If not required, check here ▶ [ ]	13	
14	Other gains or (losses). Attach Form 4797	14	
15a	IRA distributions 15a	b Taxable amount (see page 21)	15b	
16a	Pensions and annuities 16a	b Taxable amount (see page 22)	16b	
17	Rental real estate, royalties, partnerships, S corporations, trusts, etc. Attach Schedule E	17	
18	Farm income or (loss). Attach Schedule F	18	
19	Unemployment compensation	19	
20a	Social security benefits 20a	b Taxable amount (see page 24)	20b	
21	Other income. List type and amount (see page 24)	21	
22	Add the amounts in the far right column for lines 7 through 21. This is your **total income** ▶	22	1,353

Adjusted Gross Income

23	Educator expenses (see page 26)	23	
24	Certain business expenses of reservists, performing artists, and fee-basis government officials. Attach Form 2106 or 2106-EZ	24	
25	Health savings account deduction. Attach Form 8889	25	
26	Moving expenses. Attach Form 3903	26	
27	One-half of self-employment tax. Attach Schedule SE	27	95
28	Self-employed SEP, SIMPLE, and qualified plans	28	
29	Self-employed health insurance deduction (see page 26)	29	
30	Penalty on early withdrawal of savings	30	
31a	Alimony paid b Recipient's SSN ▶	31a	
32	IRA deduction (see page 27)	32	
33	Student loan interest deduction (see page 30)	33	
34	Tuition and fees deduction. Attach Form 8917	34	
35	Domestic production activities deduction. Attach Form 8903	35	
36	Add lines 23 through 31a and 32 through 35	36	95
37	Subtract line 36 from line 22. This is your **adjusted gross income** ▶	37	1,258

For Disclosure, Privacy Act, and Paperwork Reduction Act Notice, see page 83. | Cat. No. 11320B | Form **1040** (2007)

Now things should be very familiar again if you have reviewed and understood the previous tax sections in this book. Complete the Form 1040 through Line 57. (Use the previous instructions if needed.)

Do you have $1,645 on Line 40, Standard Deduction? (You needed to use Form 1040, Line 12 for your earned income amount.) Check if your dependent worksheet looks like this:

Standard Deduction Worksheet for Dependents—Line 40		*Keep for Your Records*
Use this worksheet **only** if someone can claim you, or your spouse if filing jointly, as a dependent.		

1.	Is your **earned income*** more than $550? ☒ Yes. Add $300 to your earned income. Enter the total ☐ No. Enter $850	.... **1.** **1,645**
2.	Enter the amount shown below for your filing status. • Single or married filing separately—$5,350 • Married filing jointly—$10,700 • Head of household—$7,850	.... **2.** **5,350**
3.	**Standard deduction.**	
	a. Enter the **smaller** of line 1 or line 2. If born after January 1, 1943, and not blind, **stop here** and enter this amount on Form 1040, line 40. Otherwise, go to line 3b .... **3a.**	**1,645**
	b. If born before January 2, 1943, or blind, multiply the number on Form 1040, line 39a, by $1,050 ($1,300 if single or head of household) .... **3b.**	
	c. Add lines 3a and 3b. Enter the total here and on Form 1040, line 40 .... **3c.**	

* **Earned income** includes wages, salaries, tips, professional fees, and other compensation received for personal services you performed. It also includes any amount received as a scholarship that you must include in your income. Generally, your earned income is the total of the amount(s) you reported on Form 1040, lines 7, 12, and 18, minus the amount, if any, on line 27.

Did you have 0 on Line 57? This is correct.

You will see you already made an entry on Line 58 for your self-employment tax of $190.

Line 63 tells you to add lines 57 through 62, so enter $190.

Line 64 is the Federal Income Tax withheld on your Form W-2. You had no W-2 so leave this line blank.

Line 65 through 71, do not apply to children. Skip to Line 72 and do the math. The answer is zero. Leave Line 72 blank.

Line 73 says if Line 72 is more than Line 63, subtract … but it's not. Actually Line 63 is *more* than Line 72! Leave Line 73 blank and go to Line 76.

Line 76 says to subtract Line 72 from Line 63 and we arrive at $190 on a line that says, *Amount you owe.* Ugh! What happened? What did we do wrong? Did we make a mistake? Your Form 1040 shows you owe taxes to the IRS!

The Back of your Form 1040 back should look like this:

Tax and Credits

Line	Description	Amount
38	Amount from line 37 (adjusted gross income)	1,258
39a	Check if: ☐ You were born before January 2, 1943, ☐ Blind. ☐ Spouse was born before January 2, 1943, ☐ Blind. Total boxes checked ▶ 39a	
b	If your spouse itemizes on a separate return or you were a dual-status alien, see page 31 and check here ▶39b ☐	
40	Itemized deductions (from Schedule A) or your **standard deduction** (see left margin)	1,645
41	Subtract line 40 from line 38	-387
42	If line 38 is $117,300 or less, multiply $3,400 by the total number of exemptions claimed on line 6d. If line 38 is over $117,300, see the worksheet on page 33	0
43	Taxable income. Subtract line 42 from line 41. If line 42 is more than line 41, enter -0-	0
44	Tax (see page 33). Check if any tax is from: a ☐ Form(s) 8814 b ☐ Form 4972 c ☐ Form(s) 8889	0
45	Alternative minimum tax (see page 36). Attach Form 6251	
46	Add lines 44 and 45 ▶	0

Standard Deduction for—

• People who checked any box on line 39a or 39b or who can be claimed as a dependent, see page 31.

• All others:

Single or Married filing separately, $5,350

Married filing jointly or Qualifying widow(er), $10,700

Head of household, $7,850

Line	Description		Amount
47	Credit for child and dependent care expenses. Attach Form 2441	47	
48	Credit for the elderly or the disabled. Attach Schedule R	48	
49	Education credits. Attach Form 8863	49	
50	Residential energy credits. Attach Form 5695	50	
51	Foreign tax credit. Attach Form 1116 if required	51	
52	Child tax credit (see page 39). Attach Form 8901 if required	52	
53	Retirement savings contributions credit. Attach Form 8880	53	
54	Credits from: a ☐ Form 8396 b ☐ Form 8859 c ☐ Form 8839	54	
55	Other credits: a ☐ Form 3800 b ☐ Form 8801 c ☐ Form___	55	
56	Add lines 47 through 55. These are your total credits	56	0
57	Subtract line 56 from line 46. If line 56 is more than line 46, enter -0- ▶	57	0

Other Taxes

Line	Description	Amount
58	Self-employment tax. Attach Schedule SE	190
59	Unreported social security and Medicare tax from: a ☐ Form 4137 b ☐ Form 8919	
60	Additional tax on IRAs, other qualified retirement plans, etc. Attach Form 5329 if required	
61	Advance earned income credit payments from Form(s) W-2, box 9	
62	Household employment taxes. Attach Schedule H	
63	Add lines 57 through 62. This is your **total tax** ▶	190

Payments

If you have a qualifying child, attach Schedule EIC.

Line	Description		Amount
64	Federal income tax withheld from Forms W-2 and 1099	64	
65	2007 estimated tax payments and amount applied from 2006 return	65	
66a	Earned income credit (EIC)	66a	
b	Nontaxable combat pay election ▶	66b	
67	Excess social security and tier 1 RRTA tax withheld (see page 59)	67	
68	Additional child tax credit. Attach Form 8812	68	
69	Amount paid with request for extension to file (see page 59)	69	
70	Payments from: a ☐ Form 2439 b ☐ Form 4136 c ☐ Form 8885	70	
71	Refundable credit for prior year minimum tax from Form 8801, line 27	71	
72	Add lines 64, 65, 66a, and 67 through 71. These are your **total payments** ▶	72	

Refund

Direct deposit? See page 59 and fill in 74b, 74c, and 74d, or Form 8888.

Line	Description	Amount
73	If line 72 is more than line 63, subtract line 63 from line 72. This is the amount you **overpaid**	
74a	Amount of line 73 you want **refunded to you.** If Form 8888 is attached, check here ▶ ☐	
b	Routing number ▶ c Type: ☐ Checking ☐ Savings	
d	Account number ▶	
75	Amount of line 73 you want **applied to your 2008 estimated tax** ▶ 75	

Amount You Owe

Line	Description	Amount
76	**Amount you owe.** Subtract line 72 from line 63. For details on how to pay, see page 60 ▶	190
77	Estimated tax penalty (see page 61) 77	

Third Party Designee

Do you want to allow another person to discuss this return with the IRS (see page 61)? ☐ Yes. Complete the following. ☐ No

Designee's name ▶   Phone no. ▶ ( )   Personal identification number (PIN) ▶

Sign Here

Joint return? See page 13. Keep a copy for your records.

Under penalties of perjury, I declare that I have examined this return and accompanying schedules and statements, and to the best of my knowledge and belief, they are true, correct, and complete. Declaration of preparer (other than taxpayer) is based on all information of which preparer has any knowledge.

Your signature	Date	Your occupation	Daytime phone number
YOUR SIGNATURE	DATE	STUDENT	(YOUR PHONE
Spouse's signature. If a joint return, both must sign.	Date	Spouse's occupation	

Paid Preparer's Use Only

Preparer's signature ▶	Date	Check if self-employed ☐	Preparer's SSN or PTIN
Firm's name (or yours if self-employed), address, and ZIP code ▶		EIN	
		Phone no. ( )	

Form **1040** (2007)

How can that be? Your best friend working at the Pizza shop is receiving a refund! You want a refund too! But you have a $190 bill! You may feel like this book was no help at all. Self-employment is not worth it. You may be very frustrated at the moment. What was the point? And more importantly, how are *you* going to pay this bill?

Take a deep breath. It's ok. This will happen and now that you know about it, now that you are educated, you can plan for it. Remember the farmer from *The Decision* chapter who is educated and plans for his tomatoes so he has no worries about the frost. That will be you. You are now educated about what to expect at tax time. At tax time, you will not be like the surprised farmer who did not know about the frost. That will not be you because you have this book. You are educated and know what to expect with self-employment.

Let's explain further. Let's think about why you owe on your tax return.

You were making money all through the year but you never paid your Social Security or Medicare taxes. Your friend who worked at the pizza shop had an employer who withheld Medicare, Social Security, and federal taxes. Her employer reduced her paychecks by these amounts. This is why your friend does not owe taxes! She received a refund because she had too much withheld in federal taxes. Her refund had nothing to do with Social Security and Medicare. She does not owe on her tax return because she was paying her Social Security and Medicare each time she worked, each time her paycheck was reduced.

Should you be jealous that she has money and you are stuck with this bill? Maybe, after all no one likes to pay a bill.

But if you plan accordingly, you will save extra money each year in your savings account so you can pay your taxes due. The taxes you owe are actually Social Security and Medicare.

"It's still a lot of money," you tell me.

Yes, the amount is large, especially since you are paying it in a big lump sum like this. But remember we are using a large salary in our example. We said you earned $1,370 in babysitting money. (Many babysitters earn under $400 a year so they would owe no taxes.) When you earn a large salary, expect a larger tax bill. As you earn more, you will owe more.

But is it worth it? Yes, because the tax-free wealth that compounds in your Roth IRA is much more important than the self-employment tax due each year.

Here is another reason it is worth being self-employed. Power! You are your own boss. When you have the Pizza job, you must show up when your boss says. If you are your own boss babysitting, you are able to decide your work hours. You have full control. That is good. That is *power*!

You will appreciate this when there is a party Friday night and you can go but your best friend has to come late because she is working. You can go because you set your own hours. How very nice it is… to be the boss!

Now that you understand and believe your taxes are accurate, sign, date, make a copy of your forms for your records, and mail in your Form 1040, Schedule C, and Schedule SE, along with a check for the balance due.

If you still only have a savings account, give your parents money from your savings account and ask them to write a check payable to the IRS for the balance due.

Wow! We did a lot! It was probably very uncomfortable because we are not used to it and in this case it was a little difficult because we had to use three forms. Use this example year after year to help complete your taxes.

You may ask me, "Will I always owe when I am self-employed?" Yes, usually you will owe money because no Social Security or Medicare taxes are withheld. There is no avoiding this fact. As you grow older, you may qualify for some of the tax credits (those lines we skipped) on the back of the form and these credits could result in contributing toward a refund. Then it could happen that you will not owe taxes. But as a safe bet, just expect to always pay a little bit while you are self-employed with a low income. Save some money for your tax bill due when you file.

Now, if you are really, really low income, because you are just starting out, then you might avoid taxes as well. Remember if you make under $400 on your Schedule C, then you would not owe self-employment tax and thus not owe taxes. The $400 figure might change in the future as well, so remember to always read the *current* forms and publications.

I know I keep sending you to the publications but that is where the law is and that is your back up for doing things legally correct. A good policy for the self-employed with low income is to be sure to save some of your money in savings to pay your end of year taxes.

How do you know how much you can contribute to you Roth IRA? Well, you don't have an entry on Line 7 for wages so we cannot use the same method we used earlier. Earned income, for the self-employed, is defined as the amount on Line 12, *Business Income* of your Form 1040 *less* the amount on Line 28, *One-half self-employment income*.

In our example, that means we take $1,345 from Line 12, subtract Line 28 of $95, and arrive at $1,250. $1,250 is your earned income for the year. This is the amount you will compare with the Roth IRA limit for the year and choose which ever figure is *less*.

In this example, for tax year 2007, the maximum you can contribute to your IRA is $4,000 or your earned income, which ever is less. $1,250 is less than $4,000 so you cannot contribute more than $1,250 into your Roth IRA.

Tax Return Checklist for Self-Employed Children

- Complete Schedule C, *Profit or Loss from Business* & Jump back to enter the amount on Form 1040, Line 12
- Complete Form 1040 personal information
- Answer presidential election campaign question
- Answer filing status question
- Enter interest income from savings account
- Jump—complete Schedule SE, *Self-Employment Tax* & Jump back to enter the amount on Line 58 of the Form 1040 and half the amount on Line 27 of the Form 1040
- Use the *Standard Deduction Worksheet for Dependents* (see 1040 instructions) to compute your deduction amount
- If needed, look up the tax on your taxable income
- Do the math to see if you have a refund or taxes due
- Review Roth IRA contributions for the year
- Update your Roth IRA contribution sheet (see appendix)
- Complete state and local taxes with a parent's help

IRS Publications that May Help with Tax Returns for Self-Employed Children

- Form 1040 *U.S. Individual Income Tax Return Instructions*
- Publication 334, *Tax Guide for Small Businesses*
- Publication 525, *Taxable and Nontaxable Income*
- Publication 535, *Business Expenses*
- Publication 583, *Starting a Business and Keeping Records*
- Publication 587, *Business Use of Your Home*
- Publication 590, *Individual Retirement Arrangements*
- Publication 929, *Tax Rules for Children and Dependents*
- Schedule C, *Profit or Loss from Business Instructions*
- Schedule SE, *Self-Employment Tax Form Instructions*
- *What is Taxable and Nontaxable Income*, IRS article

Taxes for Job Type 4: Self-Employed Child Selling Products

(Tax instructions build on previous tax instructions, so please read prior sections before continuing here.)

We have learned that self-employment is more complex than a typical job but we also learned that it can be done if you read carefully, follow the instructions, and do the math.

Now, it's time to look at how taxes are done if you sell a product. Examples could be if you are an artist and sell paintings, sell lemonade, or you sew quilts for sale. In general if you sell products, you should probably seek expert advice from your parent's tax advisor. But we can still prepare your return and then you can have it reviewed. This may reduce the cost for tax advice because most of the work will be done.

Speaking of tax advice, since you are self-employed, you will be able to deduct the tax preparation fees you would pay a tax professional for the business portion of your tax return. You can deduct the fee as an expense on the following year's taxes on Schedule C, Line 17, *Legal and Professional Services.*

> *Example:* You love to paint. You have been painting since age 3 and decided earlier this year you will sell paintings. Also, your little sister is a crafty girl and she makes beaded earrings. You know people would buy these also, so you decided to buy 20 pairs of earrings from your little sister for $5 each. You did not take a loan but used money you received from selling your paintings. You earned $8.32 in interest in your bank savings account.

Oh… There's a lot going on here! This is why in general for product selling you need to consult a tax professional for advice. (Also, we are not going to be concerned with your little sister's business income at this point. Remember she is selling products too. Let's just focus on your income.)

Where do we start? We start where we always did. We start by having good work records! When you are self-employed selling a product, you use the *Expense Sheet* and the *Sales Sheet* discussed earlier and provided in the appendix of this book.

Let's pretend this is what happened during your 2007 year:
- Jan 5: You purchased your $25 business license
- Feb 5: You purchased $65 in paints
- Mar 8: You sold 1 painting for $500
- Apr 3: You purchased 20 pairs of earrings at $5 each for a total of $100
- May 8: You sold 5 pairs of earrings at $12 each for a total of $60
- Oct 5: You sold 3 more paintings for a total of $891

Your completed *Sales* and *Expense Sheet*s would look like:

EXPENSE SHEET – Staple Receipts to the back

Date Incurred	Date Paid	Expense Amount	Expense Description	Expense Category
1/5/07	1/5/07	$ 25	Business License	License fee
2/5/07	2/5/07	$ 65	Paints & Canvas	Materials
4/3/07	4/3/07	$100	20 Earrings	Purchases

SALES SHEET _____ (write your name and job here)

Date	Item Sold	# Sold	Total Received	Cost of Goods Sold	Profit
3/8/07	Painting	1	$ 500	$ 14	$ 486
5/8/07	Earrings	5	$ 60	$ 25	$ 35
10/5/07	Painting	3	$ 891	$ 42	$ 849
			$1,451	$ 81	$1,370

Let's try and complete the taxes now. As in the prior section we will begin with the *Schedule C, Profit or Loss from Business.*

Complete A through E. (Refer to prior section if you have questions on this general information.)

Line F, *Accounting Method:* The accounting method is different from the previous example. If you have inventory, which you do because you have your sister's earrings, you most likely are going to be using the accrual method. Check Box 2, for accrual method. The accrual method means you record income and expense when it occurs even if you did not receive or pay it at that time.

If you ordered paint in December but it was on back order, so you received it in January and actually paid the bill in January. The expense is still a December expense.

Another example would be if you order 20 additional earrings from your little sister in December, you record that expense in December, even if you are not going to pay her until she finishes in March!

The general rule to remember for accrual basis accounting is to log the entry on the day you commit to buying or selling it, regardless if money was actually paid or received.

Line G wants to know if you materially participated in the operation of the business. Check "yes" because you did. It is your business and no one else works in it but you.

For Line H, check the box if you started your business this year. (In later years, you will leave this box unchecked.)

Part I, Income: This section is about income so we can expect to use our *Sales Sheet* paperwork. Again, we see the importance of keeping good records.

Line 1 is *Gross Receipts or Sales.* If you have more than one *Sales Sheet*, run a total of all the amounts received to arrive at the total amount you received this year. Enter this amount on Line 1 for your *Gross Receipts*. For our example, enter $1,451.

Line 2 is for *Returns and Allowances*. Since everyone loved your items, you had no returns. Leave this line blank.

Line 3 is a math computation and as we subtract Line 2, which is 0 we end up with $1,451 on Line 3.

Line 4 refers to *Cost of Goods Sold* and tells you to go to the back of the Schedule C. This line is asking how much it cost you for the products you sold. If you look at your *Sales Sheet*, you can run a total down the column and you arrive at $81 for the cost of the goods you sold. So, you know how much Line 4 should say. Now it is just a matter of reporting things correctly. How do we report the $81 on this form?

> Note: When you sell paintings or anything else you *make*, you will have to figure out how much the painting cost you in materials and supplies. We are pretending it cost $14 for each painting which would include the cost of canvas and the cost of the paint used on that particular painting. In your situation, you may need to consult a tax expert for help. This book only gives a general overview on selling products.

Line 4 says to use the figure from Line 42 on page 2. Flip the Schedule C over to side two and look at *Part III, Cost of Goods Sold* which is the section ending on Line 42. We have to answer lines 33 through 42 on the back of the form before going to Line 5 on the front.

Line 33 asks what method you are using to sell your products. When you pay your sister $5 and sell each set of earrings for $12, your profit is $7 on each pair. This profit is based on the cost of the item. Write an X in Box A, *Cost*.

Line 34 asks if there were changes between last year and this year in inventory. Check *No*.

Line 35, *Beginning Inventory*: If it is your first year, you will write 0. (If it is your second year, look at last years Schedule

C, Line 41, *Ending Inventory*, and see what your ending inventory value was. (Your beginning inventory should usually match your ending inventory from the year before.)

Line 36, *Purchases:* You didn't take any inventory out for personal use, so look at your *Expense Sheet* and add up any *purchase* lines. These are lines that have purchase in the category column. You have $100 from when you purchased the earrings for resale. Write $100 on Line 36. (Note: Do not count material purchases used to make goods for sale.)

Line 37, *Labor* is zero. You are not paying anyone for *their labor*. (You also do not pay yourself for your labor.)

Line 38 is *Materials and Supplies* used to make your business products. This type of supply becomes part of inventory. Look at your *Expense Sheet* and add up your purchases related to products you make. Write $65 on Line 38.

Line 39, *Other Costs*, will be blank because there are no other costs on your *Expense Sheet*.

Line 40, add Line 35 through 39 and write $165.

Line 41, *Inventory at the end of year*, asks for the value of your inventory at the end of the year. You should have 15 pairs of earrings because we bought 20 and sold 5. You have 15 earrings left worth $5 each so they are worth $75. You also have materials left to make more paintings. These paints and canvas are included in inventory as well. You bought $65 in paint. We estimated the cost of your sold paintings to be $56. The remainder of the money spent on paint is probably still left over in your art room. You should have $9 worth of supplies left ($65 - $56 = $9). We add $75 in earrings + $9 in paint to arrive at $84. Write $84 on Line 41.

On Line 42 we do the math and arrive at $81 for the *Cost of Goods Sold*. This is what we expected. It matches what we show on your sales sheet. Line 42 also says to enter this figure on Line 4 on the *front* of the Schedule C Form. Write $81 on Line 42 and also Line 4 of the Schedule C.

The back of the Schedule C should look like this:

Part III   Cost of Goods Sold (see page C-7)

33	Method(s) used to value closing inventory: a ☒ Cost b ☐ Lower of cost or market c ☐ Other (attach explanation)		
34	Was there any change in determining quantities, costs, or valuations between opening and closing inventory? If "Yes," attach explanation . . . . ☐ Yes ☒ No		
35	Inventory at beginning of year. If different from last year's closing inventory, attach explanation . .	35	0
36	Purchases less cost of items withdrawn for personal use	36	100
37	Cost of labor. Do not include any amounts paid to yourself	37	0
38	Materials and supplies	38	65
39	Other costs	39	0
40	Add lines 35 through 39	40	165
41	Inventory at end of year	41	84
42	**Cost of goods sold.** Subtract line 41 from line 40. Enter the result here and on page 1, line 4 . .	42	81

Part IV   Information on Your Vehicle. Complete this part **only** if you are claiming car or truck expenses on line 9 and are not required to file Form 4562 for this business. See the instructions for line 13 on page C-4 to find out if you must file Form 4562.

43   When did you place your vehicle in service for business purposes? (month, day, year) ▶ ....../....../......

44   Of the total number of miles you drove your vehicle during 2007, enter the number of miles you used your vehicle for:

a   Business ....   b   Commuting (see instructions)   c   Other ....

45   Do you (or your spouse) have another vehicle available for personal use?. . . . . ☐ Yes ☐ No

46   Was your vehicle available for personal use during off-duty hours? . . . . ☐ Yes ☐ No

47a   Do you have evidence to support your deduction? . . . . ☐ Yes ☐ No

  b   If "Yes," is the evidence written? . . . . ☐ Yes ☐ No

Part V   Other Expenses. List below business expenses not included on lines 8–26 or line 30.

....	
....	
....	
....	
....	
....	
....	
....	

48   Total other expenses. Enter here and on page 1, line 27 . . . . | 48 | |

The rest of the Schedule C is just like the last section. Complete Line 5. Subtract Line 4 of $81 from Line 3 of $1451 and enter $1,370 on Line 5.

Line 6 is *Other Income*. Did you receive any other income? Not in our example, so leave this blank.

Line 7 is math again. Enter $1,370 for your Gross Income.

Section II, Expenses: Look at your *Expense Sheet*. Enter the license fees of $25 on Line 23, *Taxes and Licenses*. The other items on your *Expense Sheet* do not fall into these categories because they were related to actual goods sold. We already accounted for these expenses on the reverse of the form.

On Line 28, you total up all expenses and write $25.

For Line 29, we subtract $25 on Line 28 from $1,370 on Line 7 and write $1,345 on Line29.

Line 30 refers to using part of your home for your business, for example, if you had a home office. Leave this line blank.

Line 31: Subtract Line 30 which is "0", write $1,345. We are going to take this same amount and enter it on Line 12, *Business Income* of our Form 1040. (You know this because it says so in the tiny print on the form.)

Line 32 concerns a business loss which this book does not address. If you have a loss, consult a tax professional.

Part IV, Information on your Vehicle: This is about your vehicle (car or truck) used for business. When you have a car that you use for business (a car that you pay the expenses on), you can keep track of your miles and deduct this as an expense. You would keep track of the miles driven on each trip and multiply it by a standard mileage rate set by the IRS each year. The mileage rate adjusts every year with inflation.

Part V, Other Expenses: If you had expenses that did not fall into one of the categories on the front of the form, you would list them here and then, enter the sum of all other expenses on the front of the Schedule C onto Line 27.

The front of the Schedule C looks like this:

SCHEDULE C (Form 1040)	**Profit or Loss From Business**	OMB No. 1545-0074
Department of the Treasury Internal Revenue Service (99)	(Sole Proprietorship) ▶ Partnerships, joint ventures, etc., must file Form 1065 or 1065-B. ▶ Attach to Form 1040, 1040NR, or 1041. ▶ See Instructions for Schedule C (Form 1040).	20**07** Attachment Sequence No. **09**

Name of proprietor **YOUR FIRST AND LAST NAME HERE**
Social security number (SSN) **YOUR # HERE**

A Principal business or profession, including product or service (see page C-2 of the instructions) **YOUR JOB DESCRIPTION (example: Child Care)**
B Enter code from pages C-8, 9, & 10 ▶ 4 5 3 2 2 0

C Business name. If no separate business name, leave blank.
D Employer ID number (EIN), if any

E Business address (including suite or room no.) ▶ **YOUR STREET ADDRESS**
City, town or post office, state, and ZIP code **YOUR CITY, YOUR STATE   ZIPCODE**

F Accounting method: (1) ☐ Cash (2) ☒ Accrual (3) ☐ Other (specify) ▶
G Did you "materially participate" in the operation of this business during 2007? If "No," see page C-3 for limit on losses ☒ Yes ☐ No
H If you started or acquired this business during 2007, check here ▶ ☒

Part I   Income

1	Gross receipts or sales. **Caution.** If this income was reported to you on Form W-2 and the "Statutory employee" box on that form was checked, see page C-3 and check here ▶ ☐	**1** 1,451
2	Returns and allowances	**2** 0
3	Subtract line 2 from line 1	**3** 1,451
4	Cost of goods sold (from line 42 on page 2)	**4** 81
5	**Gross profit.** Subtract line 4 from line 3.	**5** 1,370
6	Other income, including federal and state gasoline or fuel tax credit or refund (see page C-3).	**6** 0
7	**Gross income.** Add lines 5 and 6 ▶	**7** 1,370

Part II   Expenses. Enter expenses for business use of your home only on line 30.

8	Advertising	**8**	18	Office expense	**18**
9	Car and truck expenses (see page C-4).	**9**	19	Pension and profit-sharing plans	**19**
10	Commissions and fees	**10**	20	Rent or lease (see page C-5):	
11	Contract labor (see page C-4)	**11**	a	Vehicles, machinery, and equipment	**20a**
12	Depletion	**12**	b	Other business property	**20b**
13	Depreciation and section 179 expense deduction (not included in Part III) (see page C-4)	**13**	21	Repairs and maintenance	**21**
			22	Supplies (not included in Part III)	**22**
			23	Taxes and licenses	**23** 25
			24	Travel, meals, and entertainment:	
14	Employee benefit programs (other than on line 19).	**14**	a	Travel	**24a**
			b	Deductible meals and entertainment (see page C-6)	**24b**
15	Insurance (other than health)	**15**	25	Utilities	**25**
16	Interest:		26	Wages (less employment credits)	**26**
a	Mortgage (paid to banks, etc.)	**16a**	27	Other expenses (from line 48 on page 2)	**27**
b	Other	**16b**			
17	Legal and professional services	**17**			

28	**Total expenses** before expenses for business use of home. Add lines 8 through 27 in columns ▶	**28**	25
29	Tentative profit (loss). Subtract line 28 from line 7	**29**	1,345
30	Expenses for business use of your home. Attach **Form 8829**	**30**	
31	Net profit or (loss). Subtract line 30 from line 29. • If a profit, enter on both **Form 1040, line 12,** and **Schedule SE, line 2,** or on **Form 1040NR, line 13** (statutory employees, see page C-7). Estates and trusts, enter on Form 1041, line 3. • If a loss, you **must** go to line 32.	**31**	1,345
32	If you have a loss, check the box that describes your investment in this activity (see page C-7). • If you checked 32a, enter the loss on both **Form 1040, line 12,** and **Schedule SE, line 2,** or on **Form 1040NR, line 13** (statutory employees, see page C-7). Estates and trusts, enter on Form 1041, line 3. • If you checked 32b, you **must** attach **Form 6198.** Your loss may be limited.	**32a** ☐ All investment is at risk. **32b** ☐ Some investment is not at risk.	

For Paperwork Reduction Act Notice, see page C-8 of the instructions.   Cat. No. 11334P   Schedule C (Form 1040) 2007

Next complete your Schedule SE and your Form 1040 using prior instructions if needed. (The forms will look exactly like those in the last scenario because of the figures we are using.) The rule for your IRA contribution limit is also the same.

Tax Return Checklist for Self-Employed Children

- Complete Schedule C, *Profit or Loss from Business* & Jump back to enter the amount on Form 1040, Line 12
- Complete Form 1040 personal information
- Answer presidential election campaign question
- Answer filing status question
- Enter interest income from savings account
- Jump — complete Schedule SE, *Self-Employment Tax* & Jump back to enter the amount on Line 58 of the Form 1040 and half the amount on Line 27 of the Form 1040
- Use the *Standard Deduction Worksheet for Dependents* (see 1040 instructions) to compute your deduction amount
- If needed, look up the tax on your taxable income
- Do the math to see if you have a refund or taxes due
- Review Roth IRA contributions for the year
- Update your Roth IRA contribution sheet (see appendix)
- Complete state and local taxes with a parent's help

IRS Publications that May Help with Tax Returns for Self-Employed Children

- Form 1040 *U.S. Individual Income Tax Return Instructions*
- Publication 334, *Tax Guide for Small Businesses*
- Publication 525, *Taxable and Nontaxable Income*
- Publication 535, *Business Expenses*
- Publication 583, *Starting a Business and Keeping Records*
- Publication 587, *Business Use of Your Home*
- Publication 590, *Individual Retirement Arrangements*
- Publication 929, *Tax Rules for Children and Dependents*
- Schedule C, *Profit or Loss from Business Instructions*
- Schedule SE, *Self-Employment Tax Form Instructions*
- *What is Taxable and Nontaxable Income*, IRS article

How Parent Employers Provide a Form W-2 Using the Internet

Let's talk about how parents will provide a Form W-2. They should order IRS *Instructions for Forms W-2 and W-3* which has a section about completing Forms W-2 online. This is the easiest way to provide a Form W-2 and the method we will discuss in this book.

To use the online website, parents will need:

- Internet access
- A web browser with 128-bit encryption and cookies enabled
- Adobe Acrobat Reader (version 5.0 or higher recommended) which is free from **www.adobe.com**

The very first step is for parents to complete online, a one time registration process to set up a password and receive a PIN (Personal Identification Number).

Parents need the following information to register:

- Name as it appears on their Social Security card
- Social Security Number
- Date of birth
- Preferred mailing address
- Work phone number
- Fax number (optional)
- E-mail address
- Company's Employer Identification Number (EIN)
- Company or business name
- Company phone number

When the above information is available, it is time to register.

IRS *Instructions for Forms W-2 and W-3* direct employers to visit **www.socialsecurity.gov/employer** online.

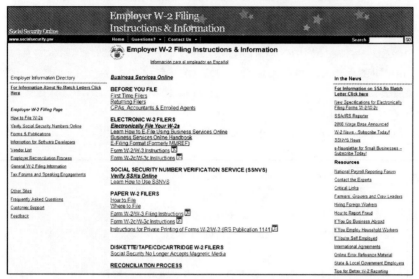

On this site employers (parents) will find all they need to create a Form W-2. Filing is free, fast, and secure. There is a lot of information on this site and parents should not become overwhelmed by all the links.

The screenshot above may change. We are looking for the section "ELECTRONIC W-2 FILERS" which should be in the middle of the page. This is the section to produce the Form W-2. We will briefly explain the available choices:

- *Electronically File Your W-2s* - takes us to *Business Services Online*, where we will register and create the Form W-2.

- *Learn How to E-File Using Business Services Online* - will bring us to a software demo and a tutorial link to a list of tutorials. Print the tutorial called *W-2 Online* (a 32 page tutorial at the time this book is being written). It has screen shots and clear instructions that you will need.

- *Business Services Online Handbook* - will take us to the handbook (which is different from the tutorial).

- *E-Filing Format* – takes us to forms and publications.
- *Form W-2/W-3 Instructions* - takes us to current IRS instructions for these forms, which we should already have since this book suggests ordering them from the IRS.
- *FormW-2c/W-3c Instructions* - takes us to instructions for these "C" forms which are correction forms one uses if a mistake was made on an original Form W-2.

We are not going to cover all the links in this book, especially since websites change so frequently. Feel free to click around the site, and read more information but we are going to focus on the essential steps to complete a Form W-2.

Register: The first step is to register. Employers (parents) set up a password and are assigned a PIN. Go to the home page:

www.socialsecurity.gov/employer

Click on *Electronically File Your W-2s* which will bring us to the Business Services Online page:

www.ssa.gov/bso/bsowelcome.htm

Look in the middle of the page and click *Register*.

On the page that opens up next, parents read the agreement and click on *I Agree* (if they agree). They answer the registration questions and again click the *Register* button.

Next if parents have not printed the W-2 Online tutorial, they should do so because the tutorial has screen images and instructions that will be used to produce the Form W-2. To print the tutorial, parents should first try this link:

www.ssa.gov/employer/W-2%20Online.pdf

If that link has gone out of date, as often happens on the internet, go back to **www.socialsecurity.gov/employer** and this time, choose *Learn How to E-File Using Business Services Online.* On the next page, choose *Business Services Online Tutorial* and on the following page, choose *W-2 Online,* being careful not to choose "text only" because then the screen shot images will not be included in your instructions.

Once parents have the *W-2 Online Tutorial Instructions,* their password, and their PIN, they can now produce a Form W-2 for their child. Use the tutorial instructions now.

Let's go back to: **www.ssa.gov/bso/bsowelcome.htm**

This time parents will click on the *Login* button and follow their printed tutorial instructions. The employer information is the parent's information and the employee information is their child's information. Parents should continue using the tutorial instructions to finish creating the Form W-2.

Further help can be found in *Instructions for Forms W-2* and from *Business Services Online* at 1-800-772-6270. This book cannot cover line by line submission details as websites often change. Instead parents need to refer to the BSO Tutorial as *Business Services Online* should keep that information current.

Parents should create a Form W-2 for each child employee and a summary, Form W-3, combining all Forms W-2. Copies should be printed for business records and for each child employee to file with their taxes. That is the main reason we are on this site, to produce the Form W-2 that a working child needs to file taxes. We are not reporting Social Security or Medicare wages because there are none in the examples we discussed. (Other employers use this site to both produce Forms W-2 and report Social Security and Medicare wages.)

Child Employment Examples

The Movie Ticket Taker who didn't claim "Exempt"

During 2007, Michael, age 16, worked all summer and school weekends at the movie theater collecting tickets from customers. He did not claim *Exempt* on his Form W-4. At the end of the year, Michael received a Form W-2 from his employer that said his wages were $3,000.

- Will Michael have a refund, balance due, or neither?
- How much can Michael contribute to a Roth IRA?

For taxes, Michael completes the Form 1040 reporting any savings account interest plus his wages of $3,000. He did not claim *Exempt*, so federal taxes were withheld. He reports this amount on his Form 1040. Michael owes no federal tax since his income was so low (less than the amount of his standard deduction of $5,350 allowed in 2007). Upon completion of his tax return, he will have a refund from the federal government equal to the amount of his federal taxes withheld.

Michael is legally allowed to contribute $3,000 into his Roth IRA because that is his earned income and it is less than the maximum of $4,000 set by the IRS for tax year 2007.

The Movie Ticket Taker who claimed "Exempt"

During 2007, Ann, age 14, worked all summer and school weekends at the movie theater collecting tickets from customers. She claimed *Exempt* on her Form W-4. At the end of the year, Ann received a Form W-2 from her employer that said her wages were $3,000.

- Does Ann expect a refund, balance due, or neither?
- How much can Ann contribute to a Roth IRA?

For taxes, Ann completes the Form 1040 reporting any savings account interest plus wages of $3,000. She claimed

Exempt on her Form W-4, so no federal taxes were withheld. She owes no taxes, because she earned so little money (less than the amount of her standard deduction of $5,350 allowed in 2007). She has neither a balance due nor a refund.

Ann is legally allowed to contribute $3,000 into her Roth IRA because that is her earned income and it is less than the maximum of $4,000 set by the IRS for tax year 2007.

The Dog Walker

In 2007, Johnny, age 6, walked his neighbor's dog every day for a half hour. Johnny kept a receipt book (donated by his parents). He provided a receipt to his neighbor and he kept a copy for himself.

He opened a separate checking account to use only for business and deposited all the business cash received into this account. He also opened a savings account for personal money like the birthday money he received from Grandma and the $5 dollar bill he found on the street. Johnny started working in September so he did not earn much for the year. Johnny only earned $80 for the entire year.

- Does Johnny expect a refund, balance due, or neither?
- How much can Johnny contribute to a Roth IRA?

For taxes, Johnny will complete a Schedule C because he was his own employer intending to actively continue this business for a profit on a regular basis. His Schedule C will show a profit of $80 because he had no expenses.

Johnny had no self-employment tax because he earned so little money (under $400 net-profit). Johnny also owes no federal tax because his income was so low (less than the amount of his standard deduction allowed). His tax return shows neither a refund nor a balance due.

Johnny can only contribute his earned income of $80 to a Roth IRA because it is less than the $4,000 allowed by the IRS.

The Spanish Club & Tutoring Service Business

In 2007, Ryan, age 11, had excellent Spanish grades and really enjoyed Spanish. He lived in a neighborhood with many young children so he began an after school Spanish club and also offered tutoring services.

He tutored 2 children on a regular basis during the school year and 7 children came to his weekly club for a monthly fee. He earned $5,000 for the year. He used library books for the club activities which included conversation and reading. For tutoring, the children brought their school Spanish books so Ryan had no expenses for the year.

- Does Ryan expect a refund, balance due, or neither?
- How much can Ryan contribute to a Roth IRA?

For taxes, Ryan will complete a Schedule C because he was his own employer intending to actively continue this business for a profit on a regular basis. His Schedule C will show a profit of $5,000 because he had no expenses.

Ryan will have self-employment tax because he earned over $400 net-profit. He will complete the Schedule SE Form along with his Form 1040 and see his self-employment tax is $706.

Ryan will owe no federal tax because his income of $5,000 was less than the amount of his standard deduction allowed ($5,350 in 2007). But, upon completion of his Form 1040 he will see he has a balance due of $706 on his return. (This is because of his self-employment tax that must be paid.)

For Roth contribution purposes, Ryan's earned income is $4,647 ($5,000 earned - $353 one half self-employment tax = $4,647) but Ryan is only allowed to contribute $4,000 to his Roth IRA because that is the maximum limit set by the IRS for tax year 2007.

The Baker

Rebecca, age 16, handed out a flyer in her neighborhood advertising baked cookies. Her policy was for neighbors to call and order cookies 2 weeks in advance so Rebecca would have time to plan her baking schedule and it would not interfere with school work or extracurricular activities.

Rebecca's parents were very generous and did not charge Rebecca for using the oven electricity, but Rebecca had to purchase all the baking ingredients by herself. In 2007, she spent $370 on baking ingredients.

Rebecca also kept a receipt book (which cost her $2) and provided a receipt to neighbors with each delivery. She kept one copy for her business records.

She opened a separate checking account to use only for business. She also opened a savings account to save personal money, like the weekly allowance she receives.

Rebecca earned $1,000 from her baking sales for 2007.

Over the year she spent $200 on clothes and movies. She had also spent the business expenses of $2 + $370 so her checking account only has $428 at tax time. Rebecca waited until filing her taxes to put any money into her Roth IRA. She wanted her money readily available during the year because she knew she really liked to shop.

- Does Rebecca expect a refund, balance due, or neither ?
- How much can Rebecca contribute to a Roth IRA?

For taxes, Rebecca will complete a Schedule C because she was her own employer intending to continue this business for a profit on a regular basis. Her Schedule C will show a profit of $628 because she takes her sales receipts of $1,000 and subtracts her expenses of the $2 receipt book and $370 in materials.

She will complete the Schedule SE Form and learn that she owes self-employment tax of $89. Rebecca will have to use some of her $428 in her checking account to pay her $89 balance due which leaves $339 in her checking account.

Legally Maria can contribute any amount up to $583 to her IRA. ($628 business income - $45 one half self-employment tax = $583.) However, Maria will choose to contribute only $339 to her Roth IRA because that is all she has left in her account.

The Family Member Household Employee

In 2007, Jenny, age 8, cleaned the bathroom in her house almost every weekend. She missed a few weekends when she went to her friend's house for a sleep over.

The work was equivalent to work of a cleaning lady and Jenny kept a task chart that her parents signed as a record of her work. Her parents paid her $9 per job.

Jenny opened a savings account which had $457 at the end of the year. $450 was from work and $7 was from bank interest. $450 was the actual amount of her take home pay because no federal, Social Security, or Medicare taxes were withheld since she was a family household employee under age 21 and claimed *Exempt* on her Form W-4.

- Does Jenny expect a refund, balance due, or neither?
- How much can Jenny contribute to a Roth IRA?

For taxes, Jenny uses a Form 1040, reporting her $7 savings account interest plus her $450 earned wages. She has a Form W-2 her parents provided her from using *Business Services Online*. Jenny owes no federal tax because she earned so little money (less than the amount of her standard deduction allowed, $5,350 in 2007).

Jenny can legally contribute up to $450 to her Roth IRA. She decides to only contribute $68 which is 15% of the amount of her $450 earned income. She is saving the rest of her money for a future purchase. She wants a laptop computer.

The Family Member Office Assistant

In 2007, Enrique, age 17, helped his mother in her self-employment business which operated out of their home. He claimed *Exempt* on his Form W-4.

He did all sorts of odd jobs. For example: he addressed mailing labels and stuffed envelopes, he counted and unpacked inventory items, he taped up packing boxes, he labeled items with the company name, and he learned website coding so he could help in that area too. He also has his driver's license, so he used the family car to help mail customer packages at the post office.

He kept a spreadsheet of the dates and time he worked, as well as the task completed. He was paid $10 per hour and at the end of the year had earned $7,500. No Social Security or Medicare taxes were withheld since he was a family member under age 18 working in his parents business.

He has a Form W-2 his mother provided him from using *Business Services Online*. He had claimed *Exempt* on his Form W-4 because he did not think he would work much this year. Since he claimed *Exempt*, no federal taxes were withheld.

- Does Enrique expect a refund, balance due, or neither?
- How much can Enrique contribute to a Roth IRA?

For taxes, Enrique uses a Form 1040, reporting any savings account interest plus his wages of $7,500 in earned income. Enrique expects to owe some federal tax because he earned $7,500 which is more than his standard deduction allowed ($5,350 for 2007). Enrique decides he will not claim *Exempt* for 2008 because he plans to work the same hours, does not want a balance due next year, and no longer qualifies for *Exempt* status. His parents will begin withholding federal taxes.

Even though Enrique earned $7,500, he can contribute only $4,000 into his Roth IRA because that was the maximum limit set by the IRS for 2007.

Frequently Asked Questions

1) What is the age requirement to contribute to a Roth IRA?
   Answer: As long as you have earned income, you may contribute to a Roth IRA. There is no age limit.

2) How much can I contribute to a Roth IRA?
   Answer: You can contribute the amount of your earned income or the current amount set each year by the IRS, whichever is *less*.

3) Grandpa gave me $50 for my straight "A" report card. Can I contribute this $50 to a Roth IRA?
   Answer: No, you cannot. It is not earned income.

4) I just learned about the Roth IRA. In the last two years, I earned $400 each summer and I earned another $400 this year. Can I add all my earned income from the last two years, plus the $400 earned this summer and contribute $1,200 to my Roth IRA this year?
   Answer: No. Each year stands alone. You can only contribute what you earned during the current year.

5) Will I save on my current taxes with a Roth IRA?
   Answer: No. Contributions to a Roth IRA are not tax deductible. You will save taxes on the growth of the Roth IRA investment. Your earnings grow tax-free.

6) Am I guaranteed to make money with a Roth IRA?
   Answer: No. How much money your Roth earns depends on the type of Roth IRA account you choose. If you choose a risky stock that goes down in price, your Roth IRA can conceivably lose money. Choose wisely with the help of parents, friends, and advisors.

7) What do I do if I contributed too much to a Roth IRA?

   Answer: You consult a tax professional for help as penalties may be involved.

8) At what age do I have to withdraw Roth IRA money?

   Answer: There are no mandatory withdrawals (unless your Roth IRA was inherited). If you choose to make no withdrawals, at your death, your account will pass to your designated beneficiaries as an inherited IRA.

9) Do I have to leave my money in a Roth IRA for 5 years before I can withdraw it without paying taxes and a penalty on it?

   Answer: By using the term *money* you are mixing *contributions* with *earnings*. There are different rules for each. You may withdraw your contribution amounts at anytime without paying taxes or penalty. There is a 5 year rule applying to earnings that has several exceptions. Check *IRS Publication 590, Individual Retirement Accounts* or consult a tax professional. (This book discourages withdrawals before retirement age due to the loss of tax-free compounding growth.)

10) At what age are you required to file a tax return?

   Answer: There is no age requirement to file taxes. The requirement is based on income. (Even if you are not required to file a return, this book recommends you always file to ensure you do not miss a refund due to you and to document your earned income.)

11) Parents want to know, "If our children begin working, can we still claim them as a dependent?"

   Answer: Yes, you can (assuming you provide more than half of their support or meet other qualifying dependent rules set by the IRS).

Challenge Questions

1. *What if you had two Employer – Employee type jobs? What is your earned income amount used to determine how much you can contribute to your Roth IRA?*

Answer: You will have two W-2 Forms. Add both amounts from Box 1 and enter the total on Line 7 of your Form 1040. Use the Line 7 amount to compare which is less, your earned income or the yearly contribution limit.

2. *What if you were employed as a babysitter and a cashier at Pete's Pizza? What is your earned income amount used to determine how much you can contribute to your Roth IRA?*

Answer: Your Form 1040 would be a combination of an Employer – Employee type job and Self-Employed type job. This means you will have an entry on Line 7 for wages and also an entry on Line 12 for self-employment income. You may also have an entry on Line 27, One-half self-employment tax. It's as if you combined both 1040 Forms from our scenarios in this book.

For your earned income, add Line 7, *Wages*, plus Line 12, *Business Income*, and subtract out the amount on Line 27, ½ *Self-Employment Tax*. The resulting figure is your earned income, the amount to use when comparing which is less, your earned income or the contribution limit for the year.

3. *When do employed children avoid paying Social Security and Medicare taxes?*

Answer: Social Security and Medicare taxes are not due for children: under age 18 working for parents in a sole proprietorship or spouse partnership business, under age 21 working as a family household employee, or of any age when their self-employment income is less than net $400.

APPENDIX A – Income Sheet

INCOME SHEET

Date	Time In	Time Out	Task	Location	Hired By: Person & Phone	Amount paid

APPENDIX B — Expense Sheet

EXPENSE SHEET – Staple Receipts to the back

Date Incurred	Date Paid	Expense Amount	Expense Description	Expense Category

APPENDIX C — Sales Sheet for the Self-Employed

SALES SHEET

Date	Item Sold	# Sold	Total Received	Cost of Goods Sold	Profit

APPENDIX D—Household Job Description Example

Check	Task: Bathroom Cleaning
	CLEAN SINK
	Begin by clearing items off sink & preparing soapy bucket
	Clean counter & sink paying special attention to drain
	Pull out drain stopper, clean and place back in the drain
	Clean soap dish. Dry sink with clean rag
	Put items back on the sink, soap dish, air freshener, etc.
	Straighten out inside of cabinet drawers
	CLEAN TOILET
	Move trash can and plunger out of bathroom
	Clean top of back of toilet
	Use toilet brush hard underneath edge of inside of toilet.
	Clean toilet seat cover and seat, both sides
	Clean where toilet seat connects to bowl
	Clean outside of toilet to the floor, watch curvy spots!
	Empty bucket. Get new hot soapy water. Never use water used for cleaning toilet for other areas.
	CLEAN FLOOR
	Clean entire floor paying close attention to area where toilet meets the floor. Dry floor with clean rags.
	Empty trash and replace with new plastic bag
	CLEAN MIRRORS / REPLACE TOWELS
	Clean all bathroom mirrors
	Fold towels neatly, replace if needed
	SHOWER / TUB
	Clean shower - surface of doors (both sides), walls, floor.
	Clean entire tub paying close attention to any soap rings
	COMPLETED BY: **INSPECTED BY:**
	DATE COMPLETED:

APPENDIX E – Roth IRA Contribution Sheet

Date	Contribution for Year	Amount Contributed	Amount Allowed	Account Value on Dec 31

APPENDIX F — More Educational Finance Books

Early Reading Books

Alexander, Who Used to Be Rich Last Sunday by Judith Virost

A Dollar for Penny by Dr. Julie Glass

Erandi's Braids by Antonio Hernandez Madrigal

The Go-Around Dollar by Barbara Johnston Adams

It's A Habit, Sammy Rabbit! by Sam X Renick

It's Not What You've Got: Lessons for Kids on Money and Abundance by Wayne W. Dyer, K. Tracy, and S. Heller Budnick

Money, Money, Honey Bunny! by Marilyn Sadler

The Penny Pot (MathStart Series) by Stuart J Murphy

You Can't Buy a Dinosaur with a Dime by Harriet Ziefert

Tween and Teen Books

Allowance Magic by David McCurrach

The Amazing Days of Abby Hayes: Have Wheels, Will Travel by Anne Mazer

Better Than a Lemonade Stand by Daryl Bernstein

Beyond the Lemonade Stand by Bill Rancic

Career Ideas for Kids Who Like Math and Money by D. L. Reeves

The Everything Kids Money Book by Diane Mayr

Growing Money: A Complete Investing Guide for Kids by Karlitz

In Business with Mallory by Laurie Friedman

Lawn Boy by Gary Paulsen

The Little Entrepreneur Takes Flight by Harper and Arrington

Owen Foote: Money Man by Stephanie Greene

Rich Dad Poor Dad for Teens by Robert T. Kiyoski

The Rich Kid by Daniel Scott

A Smart Girls Guide to Money by Nancy Holyoke

Street Wise: A Guide for Teen Investors by Janet Bamford

The Toothpaste Millionaire by Jean Merrill

The Totally Awesome Business Book for Kids by Adriane G. Berg and Arthur Berg Bochner

The Young Investor by Katherine R. Bateman

Books for Young Adults and Parents

Beyond the Grave: The Right Way and the Wrong Way of Leaving Money to Your Children (and Others) - Gerald M. Condon

Make Your Kid a Millionaire: 11 Easy Ways Anyone Can Secure a Child's Financial Future by Kevin McKinley, CFP

Parlay Your IRA into a Family Fortune by Ed Slott

Raising Money Smart Kids: What They Need to Know about Money and How to Tell Them by Janet Bodnar

Small Time Operator, 10th Edition: How to Start Your Own Business, Keep Your Books, Pay Your Taxes & Stay Out of Trouble by Bernard B. Kamoroff

APPENDIX G — Strategy, Bargaining, & Investment Games[28]

You probably know: Monopoly, Payday, and The Game of Life. Now try:

Acquire

Cash Flow for Kids or Cash Flow 101 Board Game (college)

Decisions: A Stock Market Money Game

I'm the Boss

Moneywise Kids

The Motley Fool's Buy Low Sell High

Pit

Power Grid

Risk

Settlers of Catan – *Our #1 choice for having fun while teaching supply and demand.*

Stock Market Game at www.smgww.org

Stock Market Tycoon

Stock Rush Game

Tigris and Euphrates

Triopoly

---

[28] Up to date links for money and investment games are found at www.tracytrends.com/teach-kid-money.html

APPENDIX H — Money Related Websites[29]

Bureau of Labor Statistics at www.bls.gov/k12 allows kids to explore career possibilities based on their area of interest such as math, reading, helping people etc.

Calculator (Roth IRA) www.dinkytown.net/java/RothIRA.html helps compare tax-free accounts with regular savings accounts.

Jump Start Coalition at www.jumpstart.org/principles.cfm has a website links to lessons on the 12 principles that every young person should know.

Kids' Money at www.KidsMoney.org has a wide mixture of information ranging from banks, activities, books, games and more for parents and kids.

The Mint, It Makes Perfect Cents at www.themint.org provides basic information about starting a business, earning money, spending it wisely.

Money Instructor at www.moneyinstructor.com has a wide mixture of resources and articles.

US Mint at www.USMint.gov/kids/ has online games for kids.

US Small Business administration for Teens at ww.sba.gov/teens has a mix of valuable information for kid entrepreneurs.

Young Investor at www.younginvestor.com has articles for kids, teens, parents, and teachers about how to save money or start a business.

Youth Rules at www.youthrules.dol.gov has information for educators, parents, employers and teens, especially on rules based on a child's ages and exemptions from child labor rules.

---

[29] More websites with up to date links are found at www.tracytrends.com/teach-kid-money.html

APPENDIX I — Places To Open A Roth IRA For A Minor[30]

Charles Schwab: at www.Schwab.com, (866) 232-9890. Open a Roth IRA account for a minor with $100.

Franklin Templeton: at www.FranklinTempleton.com, (800)632-2301. Open an account at age 14 with $250 or a $50 regular monthly investment.

H&R Block Financial Advisors: at www.hrblock.com (enter your zip code to find a local advisor). Open an account through financial advisors with $1,000 or $100 plus a $100 regular monthly investment or, open through H&R Block tax professionals (when you file your taxes) with $300.

Janus: at www.Janus.com, (800)525.3713. Open an account with $1,000 or $500 plus a monthly investment.

Scottrade: at www.scottrade.com, (800)619-7283. In Nov, 2007, Scottrade was recommended by *Kiplinger's Personal Finance* magazine, for Roth accounts for minors. Open an account with $500.

T. Rowe Price: at www.TRowePrice.com, (800)541-6066. Open an account with $1,000 or a $50 regular monthly investment.

USAA Investment Management Company: for military members and their family at www.usaa.com, (800)531-8144. IRA Brokerage accounts have no minimum amount required.

Vanguard: at www.Vanguard.com, (877)662-7447. Open a custodial account with $1,000 or with a $50 regular monthly investment.

---

[30] *Amounts to open an account are subject to change. Also, be sure to ask about and compare all fees involved.*

GLOSSARY

Adjusted Gross Income (AGI): The total of all your income including paychecks, interest, other income, etc. reduced by deductions (adjustments to income) allowed by the IRS (such as ½ Self-Employment Tax or a Traditional IRA.)

Babysitting: If you baby-sit for relatives or neighborhood children, whether on a regular basis or only periodically, the rules of childcare providers apply to you.

Beneficiary: The person receiving the IRA account when the owner of the account dies.

Childcare Providers: If you provide child care, either in the child's home or in your home or other place of business, the pay you receive must be included in your income. If you are not an employee, you are probably self-employed and must include payments on form Schedule C.

Compounding Interest: Compounding interest means you will earn interest on interest you have previously earned.

Comfort Zone: How people feel about investing their money considering the investment risk and expected performance.

Contribution: The amount of earned income contributed (deposited) into an IRA for a particular tax year.

Custodial IRA Account: An IRA account opened for a minor (child under 18 or 21 depending on the state) and the parent or some other guardian is the custodian.

Dependent: Someone supported by another taxpayer. Usually (but not always) the taxpayer pays more than ½ the dependent's cost to live, including food, shelter, clothing and medical.

Dollar Cost Averaging: investing the same amount in the same investment on a regular basis for a long period of time resulting in the purchase of more shares when the price is low and fewer shares when the price is high.

Employee: has set work hours and a set job description

Employer: sets the rules for what you will do and when you will do it, writes the paychecks, and provides a form W-2.

Employer Identification Number (EIN): An Employer Identification Number (EIN) is also known as a Federal Tax Identification Number, used to identify a business entity.

Exempt Status: A status claimed on the Form W-4 claiming that you no tax liability last year and expect to have no tax liability this year.

Exemption: A legal deduction of a certain amount of income from your annual salary to avoid paying taxes on it.

Financial Stability: You do not rely on anyone for money and have emergency funds for any unforeseen events that could occur in everyday life.

Fringe Benefit: Something non-cash (like a gift) received from an employer as compensation for work performance which is considered part of your pay. Your employer generally must withhold income tax on these benefits from your regular pay.[31]

Household Employee: "You have a household employee if you hired someone to do household work and that worker is your employee. The worker is your employee if you can control not only what work is done but how it is done..."[32]

---

[31] *IRS Publication 17, Taxable Fringe Benefits*
[32] *IRS Publication 926, Household Employer's Tax Guide*

Household Work: "Household work is work done in and around your home by the following people: baby-sitters, Cleaning People, Housekeepers, Maids, Yard workers...."[33]

Interest: An amount you are paid for letting someone else use your money.

IRA: "An IRA is a personal savings plan that gives you tax advantages for setting aside money for retirement." [34]

IRA Contribution: The amount of earned income that one contributes into a Roth IRA. This can be withdrawn at any time with no penalty or taxes due on it.

IRA Contribution Limit: is the maximum amount allowed by the IRS for the applicable year or the amount of your earned income, whichever is *LESS*.

IRA Earnings: The amount of money in your IRA that exceeds your contributions. This money cannot be withdrawn before age 59½ without paying taxes and penalties.

Payroll Taxes: The amount withheld from your paycheck for Social Security and Medicare.

Required Mandatory Distributions (RMDs): A minimum amount of money you are required to withdraw annually beginning no later than April 1 of the year following the year you turn age 70½.

Self-Employed: A self-employed person provides a product or service to others with the intention of making a profit.

Self-Employment Tax: A tax paid into Social Security by self-employed persons.

---

[33] *IRS Publication 926, Household Employer's Tax Guide*
[34] *IRS Publication 590, Individual Retirement Arrangement*

Stock: A type of security representing ownership in a company.

Sole Proprietor: Someone who is in business for himself or herself and there is no other owner.

Start up money or costs: Money spent on your business before you sell products or provide your actual service.

Standard Deduction: is a dollar amount that non-itemizers may subtract from their income based upon filing status. It is available to individuals, married persons, and heads of household and increases every year. Additional amounts are available for persons 65 and over, blindness, or both.[35]

Tax Deferred: Means taxes are postponed. Taxes are not paid today but will be paid at a later date.

Unearned Income: Generally refers to income received when no work was performed. Examples applying to children might be raffle winnings or hobby income.

Withholding: The amount employers withhold from an employees paycheck for payment toward federal taxes based on the employee's completion of their Form W-4.

---

[35] www.en.wikipedia.org/wiki/Standard_deduction

Bibliography & Internet Resources

Calculator (Compound Interest):
http://www.moneychimp.com/calculator/compound_interest_calculator.htm

Calculator (Roth VS Taxable Savings):
www.dinkytown.net/java/RothIRA.html

Department of Labor at www.dol.gov

Form 1040 Instructions: Department of the Treasury Internal Revenue Service, 2006

Instructions for Forms W-2 and W-3: Wage and Tax Statement and Transmittal of Wages and Tax Statements: Department of the Treasury Internal Revenue Service, 2006

Instructions for Form W-4, Employee Withholding Allowance Certificate: Department of the Treasury Internal Revenue Service, 2007.

Internal Revenue Service (IRS) call 1-800-TAX-FORM (1-800-829-3676)

Publication 15, (Circular E), Employer's Tax Guide: Department of the Treasury Internal Revenue Service, 2007

Publication 15A, Employer's Supplemental Tax Guide (Supplement to Publication 15 (Circular E), Employers Tax Guide): Department of the Treasury Internal Revenue Service, 2007

Publication 525, Taxable and Nontaxable Income: Department of the Treasury Internal Revenue Service, 2006

Publication 334, Tax Guide for Small Business: Department of the Treasury Internal Revenue Service, 2006

Publication 501, Exemptions, Standard Deduction and Filing Information: Department of the Treasury Internal Revenue Service, 2006

Publication 525, Taxable and Nontaxable Income: Department of the Treasury Internal Revenue Service, 2006

Publication 535, Business Expenses: Department of the Treasury Internal Revenue Service, 2006

Publication 538, Accounting Periods and Method: Department of the Treasury Internal Revenue Service

Publication 583, Starting a Business and Keeping Records: Department of the Treasury Internal Revenue Service, 2007

Publication 587, Business Use of Your Home: Department of the Treasury Internal Revenue Service, 2006

Publication 590, Individual Retirement Arrangements (IRAs): Department of the Treasury Internal Revenue Service, 2006

Publication 926, Household Employer's Tax Guide: Department of the Treasury Internal Revenue Service, 2006

Publication 929, Tax Rules For Children and Dependents: Department of the Treasury Internal Revenue Service, 2006

Schedule C, Profit or Loss from Business Instructions: Department of the Treasury Internal Revenue Service, 2006

Schedule H, Household Employment Tax Instructions: Department of the Treasury Internal Revenue Service, 2006

Schedule SE, Self-Employment Tax Form Instructions: Department of the Treasury Internal Revenue Service, 2006

Stop Child Labor: at www.stopchildlabor.org

Youth Rules: at www.youthrules.dol.gov/states.htm

View Small Business Tax Workshops online or order a FREE DVD at www.irs.gov/smallbiz.

To order official IRS forms, call 1-800-TAX-FORM (1-800-829-3676) or for other IRS inquiries 1-800-829-1040

For more resources visit:

www.TracyTrends.com/teach-kid-money.html

INDEX

The author, Tracy Foote, also works as an Usborne Books at Home Educational Consultant primarily focusing on school fundraisers. When you are over 18 years old, you could do this part time job too! Visit her website:

About the Author

Tracy Foote worked in Accounting and Finance for the US Air Force. Today she is an author and a self-employed parent, who helped her own children become legally employed, so they could invest in Roth IRAs at a young age. She wrote this book to consolidate and share information to assist other employed children and their parents.

REVIEW REQUEST

If you would recommend this book to others, please consider writing a 5 star review on Amazon.com.
How to write a review in 4 easy steps:
1. On the Internet visit www.amazon.com
2. Enter 978-0-9708226-9-7 in the search box on Amazon
3. About half way down, click *Create Your Own Review*
4. Please tell others what you liked about this book

To suggest updates to this book visit:
www.TracyTrends.com/books/kid-roth-ira.html
To check for updated information on child Roth IRAs visit:
www.TracyTrends.com/books/child-roth-ira-updates.html
For more resources visit:
www.TracyTrends.com/teach-kid-money.html

EASILY ORDER THIS BOOK
- at your local bookstore
- online from **www.Amazon.com**
- from the publisher at **www.TracyTrends.com**

Printed in the United States
113936LV00003B/155/A